The FIRST WORLD WAR *Adventures of* NARIMAN KARKARIA

Celebrating
30 Years of Publishing
in India

Praise for *The First World War Adventures of Nariman Karkaria*

'*The First World War Adventures of Nariman Karkaria*, rivetingly translated by Murali Ranganathan, is unputdownable.'

– KARAN THAPAR, *Hindustan Times*

'Invaluable reading ... We have to be grateful to Murali Ranganathan for unearthing this gem and doing a superb translation.'

– RUCHIR JOSHI, *India Today*

'A series of jaunty reports from a born raconteur.'

– SANJAY SIPAHIMALANI, *Moneycontrol*

'Oscillating between two genres—war memoir and travelogue—the book ... offers a pleasurable as well as a poignant read.'

– *MargASIA*

'A must-read for scholars, historians and general readers alike ... the memoir is a piece of history to be cherished.'

– *The Telegraph*

'A stunning potpourri of a Parsi rookie soldier's experiences in the Great War, his riveting travelogue and incisive social satire, all packaged in a gung-ho, insightful translation.'

– *The Tribune*

The FIRST WORLD WAR *Adventures of* NARIMAN KARKARIA

A MEMOIR

Translated from the Gujarati by

MURALI RANGANATHAN

With a Foreword by

AMITAV GHOSH

HarperCollins *Publishers* India

First published in hardback by HarperCollins *Publishers* 2022
4th Floor, Tower A, Building No. 10, DLF Cyber City,
DLF Phase II, Gurugram, Haryana – 122002.
www.harpercollins.co.in

This edition published in India by HarperCollins *Publishers* 2023

2 4 6 8 10 9 7 5 3 1

P-ISBN: 978-93-5699-060-9
E-ISBN: 978-93-5489-358-2

Typeset in 11.5/15 Goudy Old Style at
Manipal Technologies Limited, Manipal

Printed and bound at
Thomson Press (India) Ltd

MIX
Paper
FSC FSC® C010615

This book is produced from independently certified FSC® paper to ensure responsible forest management.

Contents

The Middle Eastern Front

The Balkan Front

After the Truce

Foreword

I met Murali Ranganathan for the first time on 21 June 2011 in Mumbai, at an event for my recently published novel, *River of Smoke*, which is the second book in the *Ibis* trilogy. I had then just begun working on the last book in the trilogy, *Flood of Fire*, which is set largely in Canton (Guangzhou). When I learnt that Murali was a historian and translator, specializing in Gujarati and Marathi, I wasted no time in asking him if he knew of any nineteenth-century travel accounts of China by Parsi merchants.

To my great surprise, Murali's response was, yes, he did know of some such accounts, written in Gujarati. I was taken aback because I had been searching for such accounts for a long time and had not been able to find any (I was handicapped, of course, by my lack of Gujarati). I was initially sceptical, but Murali soon proved that he knew what he was talking about by sending me a list of travelogues written by Parsi merchants.

I was, I must admit, both disappointed and hugely impressed. The first because it was frustrating to know that these books existed but were written in a language I cannot read; the second because I knew from experience that to dig out sources like these takes real persistence and archival skill. The researchers who are equipped with the requisite abilities are almost always attached to universities, so it came as a surprise also to learn that Murali did not have any such affiliation—indeed, one of the striking things about him is that despite his immense learning, he does not seem the least bit professorial.

I soon learnt that Murali is a scholar in a much older mould, of a breed that is increasingly rare in today's highly compartmentalized world: he is an independent autodidact who has developed his formidable linguistic and archival skills largely on his own. He works on texts in Gujarati, Marathi, Urdu, Hindi, and no doubt, many other languages, and possesses a truly encyclopaedic knowledge of nineteenth-century India. What is more, his scholarly work is driven not by a desire for advancement, but by a genuine passion for the subject. If the world were a more discerning place, Murali would be a celebrated scholar, notable not only for his work, but also for the fact that he has *chosen* to be free of institutions.

A year later I was in the thick of writing *Flood of Fire*, which is, in large part, about the experiences of Indian sepoys who fought in the First Opium War. In researching the book, I discovered that even though millions of Indian sepoys fought in the armies of the British Raj, between the late eighteenth and nineteenth centuries, first-hand accounts of their experiences are vanishingly rare: indeed, the best known of them, *From Sepoy to Subedar,* may well be apocryphal. It was not till the First World War that accounts of warfare, from the sepoys' point of view, began to appear. Given the paucity of the materials, these became some of the most important background readings for *Flood of Fire.*

In the summer of 2012, I wrote to Murali hoping that he, with his extraordinary archival skills, would be able to find some accounts written by the Marathi soldiers who fought in the First

World War. Three months later, on 9 October, I received this letter from Murali:

Dear Amitav,

I have been looking for clues to answer your questions regarding Maratha soldiers and the First World War for the last few months but I have not got anywhere near answering them with any confidence.

In the meanwhile, I was also infected by travelogitis–and the only palliative was to run through as many travelogues as I could, the constraints being that they had to be from the nineteenth century and in non-English Indian languages I know. Among other things, there is something I found that could be of interest to you. Allow me to intrude on your time.

Nariman Karkaria, a young Parsi from Gujarat, had apparently always wanted to see the world. Sometime in 1910, when he was in his teens, he left home with fifty rupees in his pocket to do just that. He eventually made his way to China, travelled, among other places, to Peking and then to Japan, when somebody suggested that he might as well travel to Siberia since he was so near. And that's what he did. He eventually made his way across Siberia to St Petersburg and then on to Finland and Norway, and eventually reached London, I think, sometime in 1914 or 1915 (he is not very strong on dates). Another long-standing desire of his was to see a war and he wasn't going to let pass an opportunity which suddenly presented itself. He went to Whitehall to volunteer but they shooed him away since he was an Indian and suggested he join some desi regiment. He, however, managed to eventually register as a Private with the 24th Middlesex in its D Company, and thus became a 'Tommy', as he proudly announces.

The remaining part (about two-thirds) of the book is the typical WWI story—'No food, no water, no sleep, no relief'. Incredibly, he saw action on three fronts in the next three years. In 1916, he was at the Battle of the Somme and describes life in the trenches in vivid detail. He was lucky not to die (most of the others near him did) and was sent back to London to convalesce from an injury. After the usual recovery period and some weeks of training, he was sent off to the Middle Eastern Front where, after many trials and tribulations in Egypt, he was part of the Battle of Jerusalem (1917). He describes the triumphant entry into the city by the British forces. He was then moved to the Balkan Front where he was in Salonika with the 31st CCS; with the British Army, he later travelled through many parts of European Turkey. He was eventually discharged and returned to India after five years of travel and adventure.

He, presumably on public demand, wrote this book which was published in 1922 by D.A. Karkaria from the Manek Printing Press in Mumbai. It is deceptively titled Rangbhumi par Rakhad, *which I would translate as* Sorties on Stage. *It was perhaps intended as a pun for 'jangbhumi', a word he uses often in the text.*

In spite of the extreme trauma he endures over many pages, there is a certain Wodehousian aura which permeates the whole book. The 'stiff upper lip' is palpable and sometimes 'What ho!' is almost audible.

I must confess I have not read the book in toto but have merely flipped through it to glean the bare outlines of his career. There is much more to his book and I might be wrong with regard to details as I am writing from memory. There are many photographs both from his travels and from the war. I am not sure if he took them himself but some of them are intimate—soldiers bathing in the nude at an oasis with camels for company, for instance.

I have very little knowledge of this period or this war to be able to form a judgement about the uniqueness of this experience—an

> *Indian serving in an all-European regiment, seeing action on three major fronts of the First World War and living to tell the tale. But the book is a sure page-turner.*

I was astonished! After looking for Indian accounts of China, and of soldiering on behalf of the British Raj, for many years with very little success, here, suddenly, was a book that fitted both those bills! I wrote back: 'This is amazing! An astonishing find! Congratulations ... ! ... this is really big news (at least in my little bubble)! I will buy you a bottle of champagne some day.'

I felt from the start that the book needed to be translated and that Murali was the right person to do it. But Murali had other commitments at the time, and there were practical difficulties involved, such as finding a publisher, looking for funding, and suchlike.

So it happened that many years passed between Murali's discovery of Nariman Karkaria's *Rangbhumi par Rakhad* and the publication of *The First World War Adventures of Nariman Karkaria*. But the wait has been well worth it. Karkaria's memoir is indeed a gripping read, from the moment when he departs secretly for China, in 1910, as a boy of fifteen, and then makes his way via Hong Kong and Russia to England, where he joins up as a soldier to fight in France, Egypt, Palestine and the Balkans, ultimately returning to Mumbai via London, after the end of the war.

If there are moments when it is hard for the reader not to wonder whether Karkaria is exaggerating or fabricating, those doubts are always dispelled by his repeated mentions of exactly how much he paid for food, lodging, transportation, and so on (this remains a marked feature of Indian travel writing to this day). I, for one, do not doubt that the basic outlines of the story are true, unlikely though it may seem.

The First World War Adventures of Nariman Karkaria is in every sense a unique work, in the story that it tells, in the swashbuckling manner of its telling, and not least, in the excellence of Murali's translation, which conveys the writer's spirit so vividly that one can almost hear him reminiscing aloud to enthralled listeners at the Ripon Club in Mumbai, or the Meherjirana Library in Navsari.

Amitav Ghosh
Brooklyn
3 November 2021

Introduction

In early 1915, twenty-year-old Nariman Merwanji Karkaria, a Parsi who had been working as a shop attendant in Beijing, China, enlisted with the British Army in London to fight in the First World War. Initially attached to the 24th Middlesex Regiment as a Private and dispatched to the Western Front, Karkaria was injured in the Battle of the Somme. Upon recovery, he joined the 5th Middlesex at the Middle Eastern Front and took part in the battles that led to the conquest of Jerusalem by the Allied Forces. He was then assigned to King Edward's Horse and sent to the Balkan Front as an interpreter with the Indian Army. After the 1918 truce, his regiment was in Baku, Azerbaijan, where he was served his discharge warrant. Karkaria was likely one of the few people who had seen action on three different fronts of the Great War, as the First World War was then referred to, and had lived to tell the tale.

On his return to India in May 1920, he would have received a hero's welcome. He had returned home to Navsari, Gujarat, after nearly six years, and there were many listeners eagerly waiting for him to recount his adventures. This might have been the genesis for his column in a Gujarati newspaper chronicling his war experiences. The column was serialized from late 1920 all through 1921. The articles were then collected and published in the form of a book titled *Rangbhoomi par Rakhad*, which was published in 1922.

One part autobiography, one part travelogue, and three parts war memoir, the book manages to hold its own in a very crowded field of first-hand accounts written by soldiers who participated in the First World War. *Rangbhoomi par Rakhad* is the only Indian war memoir from the First World War to have been discovered thus far. Although the book spans the first twenty-five years of Karkaria's life, it is mainly concerned with his war experiences and associated travels. On first reading, the story seemed too fantastic to be true. Could it be the ramblings of an armchair traveller masquerading as a soldier?

While translating the book, I tried to find out a little more about the man and his motivations for writing this book. Though I did not discover much more than he cared to reveal, it was enough to convince me that much of what he recounts is based on personal experience. He may have abridged a few unpleasant experiences; he may have embroidered a few anecdotes; but this is certainly an eyewitness account, and a riveting one at that, of the First World War, written by someone who was in the line of fire. His descriptions of the war experience are indeed so immediate that one is transported to the front lines. The traumatic experiences in the trenches in France are starkly described, and the account of fighting on the hills of Palestine is exceptional.

Karkaria's story is best read in his own words, albeit in translation, and does not bear repetition here. I tried to learn a little more about his life at Navsari before the war. I was also curious about the circumstances surrounding his enlistment in the British Army and searched the military archives to unearth any records that might support his narrative. I then tried to find out a little more about his life after the war and why he slipped into obscurity after his death. While researching the book and its unique features, I also attempted to explore its relationship with Gujarati literature.

Early Life and Family

Navsari! Navsari! Navsari!

The small town of Navsari in south Gujarat is a constant refrain throughout this book. Nariman Karkaria might be buying an expensive cup of tea in Sweden or shivering in a trench on the front line, but his thoughts always seem to travel back to Navsari, the only place he could call home.

The Karkarias were one of the ancient Parsi clans who could trace their ancestry back to over four hundred years in Navsari. By the eighteenth century, Navsari had emerged as the urban focus of the Parsi community, which had settled in villages across south Gujarat. This clan considered itself important enough to publish its detailed genealogy in Gujarati, with the English title, *A Short Account of the Karkaria Family*. Printed in 1916 for private circulation, it was compiled by Kavasji Pestonji Karkaria, and contains genealogical tables and short biographical sketches of many members of the clan. Although Nariman was not yet twenty-one, he also earned an entry in the book, not for joining the British Army, but for his travel exploits before the war.

Merwanji Hormusji Karkaria, his father, was a priest who officiated in one of the many Zoroastrian fire temples that dotted the narrow lanes of Navsari. It was a hereditary position, so his sons would have been expected to continue the tradition. His religious duties would have left Merwanji with enough time to pursue other, more remunerative activities. He had a deep interest in community history and perhaps introduced Nariman to old Persian classics such as the *Shahnama*. Nariman's elder brother,

Rustom, was the Navsari correspondent of the leading Gujarati newspaper *Jame Jamshed.* Published from Mumbai since 1832, it had a wide circulation in Gujarat and among the Parsi diaspora. It was perhaps through his intercession that Karkaria's war memoir was first serialized in *Jame Jamshed.*

Although Nariman portrays himself as a truant schoolboy, the references to numerous books and historical events in the memoir suggest that he was, if not an attentive student, at least a voracious reader. The books he read certainly fired up his imagination and egged him on to seek adventures beyond Navsari. In 1910, at the age of fifteen, he decamped to China to seek his fortune. Though China was no longer the mythical Cathay, ever since the Parsis first visited China in the 1750s for trade, its reputation as a place where stupendous fortunes could be made had been cemented in Parsi lore. Karkaria's own experiences in China were very different, and his youth evoked a lot of sympathy in the well-established Parsi community in Hong Kong. A restless soul, he moved to Beijing (then known as Peking) to work with a British trading firm managed by a Parsi. He returned to India after two years but was back in Peking in 1914.

Joining the War Effort

War clouds had been gathering for most of 1914, and when British India was dragged into the war, Indian citizens were drafted in large numbers to fight for the Allied Forces. The colonial government managed to win the support of a large part of the Indian political spectrum for the war effort. The Parsi community was vociferous in its support of the British. A number of Parsi doctors, who were members of the Indian Medical Service, were drafted into military service. Others enlisted as soldiers. As an Indian, Nariman Karkaria could only have volunteered to join the Indian Army. But instead, he chose to travel to London where he hoped to join the British Army.

Karkaria's overland train journey from Peking to London via Siberia, Russia and the Scandinavian countries was an adventure that extended over many weeks. He clearly enjoyed this travel experience and recounts it with much gusto in his war memoir. When Karkaria first approached the War Office at Whitehall to enlist with the British Army, he was directed to the India Office. How, then, did he manage to join a British regiment?

The Parsis had maintained a permanent presence in the UK from the 1850s when Cama & Co., a leading Parsi trading firm based in Mumbai, sent three representatives, including Dadabhai Naoroji, to set up their UK branch. By the 1910s, a number of Parsi business houses had offices in London or Liverpool. A large number of young Parsis came to London every year to study law or to acquire degrees at Oxford or Cambridge. Two Parsis, Dadabhai Naoroji and M.M. Bhownaggree, had been elected as members of the British Parliament from London constituencies. The Parsis had evidently managed to cultivate deep connections in the UK in the previous six decades and also wielded a lot of influence in the circles of power.

But perhaps, more importantly, Karkaria's preference for a British regiment was rooted in how a section of the Parsi elite constructed their self-image. This identity, always changing, was particularly fluid in the nineteenth century. In 1800, the Parsi shipwright Jamsetjee Bomanjee (1754–1821), Master Builder of the Bombay Dockyard, built a man-of-war for the British Navy. On the keel of the ship, he carved the words, 'This ship was built by a d–d Black Fellow A. D. 1800.' When the ship was hauled up for repairs a few years later, Jamsetjee proudly pointed out the inscription. But by the start of the twentieth century, a few of them could make claims similar to what the community historian,

J.R.B. Jeejeebhoy (1885–1960), glibly did in a letter to the editor of *The Times of India* (24 August 1912): 'I may say, sir, that in our dress and manners, habits and language, we Parsis could hardly be distinguished from Europeans.' This supposition, far from reality, yet appealing, gradually came to be shared by the majority of the Parsi community.

Even before Karkaria had departed from China, a Parsi had already managed to enlist with the Middlesex Regiment in 1914. This was Karesasp Naoroji, a grandson of Dadabhai Naoroji, who was then a student at Oxford. Did Karkaria know of this before he set off for London? This does seem likely since he also joined the same regiment soon after arriving there.

I consulted numerous military archives to check if any papers relating to Nariman Karkaria had survived the numerous purges that have been undertaken in the last hundred years. A reference to the UK Public Records Office, using the regimental number he mentions in the memoir, yielded a medal card for 'Karkaria, Nawrian M'. Nariman Karkaria was awarded the Victory Medal and the British War Medal—medals issued in their millions to everyone who had seen active service in the Great War. They were so inconsequential that Karkaria does not mention them in his book.

Karkaria was constantly in touch with his family all through the war. His brother, Rustom, seems to have extracted nuggets from his letters and sent them for publication to *Jame Jamshed*. For instance, in 1916, he was hailed as the first Parsi to participate in a guard of honour for the British monarch, a dubious milestone which Karkaria skips mentioning. For the rest of the story, we have to rely on Karkaria's version of his experiences. It is unlikely that he kept a diary or even an occasional notebook during the war. While writing his weekly pieces, he seems to have largely relied on his memory and the letters he would send home, which would also have been in Gujarati; and perhaps on a scrapbook of articles that had appeared in *Jame Jamshed*, like the one describing his arrival in Hong Kong in October 1910, which he reproduces in the memoir.

A First World War Adventure

In 1920, Karkaria had no role models in the Gujarati language from whom he could draw inspiration to write a war memoir. It is a genre in which Gujarati, like most other Indian languages, has very few books even now, a century later. Karkaria therefore drew his inspiration from and modelled his narrative on the Gujarati travelogue which, by the 1920s, had developed as an important part of modern Gujarati literature. The Parsis had played a pioneering role in shaping this genre. Early narratives included Nowrozjee Furdoonjee's account of his travels in Sind, Punjab and Afghanistan in the 1830s (published in the Gujarati magazine *Juggut Premi* in 1853) and Dadabhai Naoroji's travelogue of his journey from Mumbai to London in 1855 (serialized in the Gujarati weekly *Rast Goftar*). Parsis continued to break fresh ground in travel literature with Dosabhai Framji Karaka's *Great Britain Katheni Musafari* (1861) and Ardeshir Framji Moos's *Hindustanma Musafari* (1871). By the end of the nineteenth century, even Parsi cricket clubs and theatre troupes were publishing narratives of their travels.

Perhaps the leading travel writer of the period was Jehangir Behramji Marzban (1848–1928), whose travelogues were multi-edition bestsellers. With titles such as *Mumbai thi Kashmir* (1887) and the 1906 *Modikhane thi Marsales*, the travelogues foregrounded Marzban's Parsi-ness while also describing his experiences in Europe and India. Peppered with advice to travellers who might follow in his footsteps, his text occasionally reads like a guidebook. Adopting a mildly self-deprecating tone, the accent of Marzban's turn-of-the-century travelogues was on humour. Karkaria adopted the same register as Marzban for a large part of his war memoir. It was no coincidence that Marzban's son, Pherozeshah, was the proprietor-editor of *Jame Jamshed* in which Karkaria's war memoir was first serialized in 1920–21.

The Gujarati book is titled *Rangbhoomi par Rakhad*, which translates as 'Rambles on Stage'. 'Rangbhoomi' itself translates as 'theatre', and is used in the title as a reference to the theatres of war. My first encounter with *Rangbhoomi par Rakhad* in 2012 was serendipitous. While trawling for books on Gujarati theatre at the K.R. Cama Oriental Institute in Mumbai, I came upon a copy of the book.

The book is loaded with front matter. Besides Karkaria's own preface and a note from the publisher, Dinshah Karkaria, the book has two forewords, one written in Gujarati by Pherozeshah Jehangir Marzban, the editor of *Jame Jamshed*, and another in English by Lieutenant Colonel H.E. Lavie to whom the book is dedicated. Lavie, who had seen action during the First World War and was a decorated officer, had just arrived in Mumbai to take up a military assignment. Following the sales model of the nineteenth century, the book was published by subscription, and a long list of subscribers is appended to the book. Many of the subscribers were from the extended Karkaria family.

Karkaria never provides his readers with the larger picture of the Great War, and presumably they did not need it in 1922. It is written as an eyewitness account and relies mainly on his personal experiences. He is not very good with dates either. The initial chapters are accurately dated, but as the pell-mell of war overtakes the narrative, dates are given short shrift. And if he does mention a date, the year is missing. However, as many of the events he describes are well known, a chronology can be easily worked out.

In an era when racial stereotypes were bandied about without a second thought, it would be difficult to fault Karkaria for whom the Japanese were all 'dwarfish' and Jewish women were 'muscular'. He also does not miss out on labelling his fellow Parsi brethren as 'crabby'.

A disconcerting aspect of the memoir is the complete bleaching out of individual personalities. In the course of his travels, everywhere he sought out Parsis and enjoyed their hospitality. However, only in the initial chapters are a few Parsis mentioned by name. In Peking, he had numerous Parsi colleagues; he spent a week in St Petersburg (then known as Petrograd) with a Parsi friend; and when he arrived in London, he was met by yet another Parsi acquaintance. All of them are mentioned merely in passing and never by name, and no further details are proffered. And after Karkaria enlisted in the army, he continued in the same vein. It is as if he was fighting alongside a nameless horde where nobody stood out. The Tommies are as anonymous as the Germans or the Turks. No commanding officers are mentioned by name, no fellow soldiers singled out, no idiosyncrasies highlighted, and seemingly no friendships made. Was it because he was an outsider? Or was he just exercising a writer's prerogative?

Later Life

After the Great War, the colonial government established an Indian Territorial Force, and the 11th and 12th battalions of the 2nd Bombay Pioneers were formed in 1922. They were exclusively made up of Parsi recruits and were commonly referred to as the Parsi Pioneers. As a man with substantial military experience, Nariman Karkaria joined the Parsi Pioneers as a lieutenant. It provided him with the opportunity of being directly associated with the military, which he had once joined on a lark.

Once *Rangbhoomi par Rakhad* had been published in the form of a book in 1922, it seems that Karkaria now fancied himself a travel writer and was, in fact, regarded as one by the Parsi community. The following year, he took an extended sabbatical and embarked on a long ramble around Iran, the original home of the Parsis. Karkaria evidently undertook this trip with a travelogue in mind. Funded by the Parsi community, which was keen on exploring business opportunities, Karkaria was expected to not only document his travel experiences, but also report on the living conditions of the Zoroastrians of Iran and evaluate the possibility of a reverse migration of Parsis from India to Iran.

Weighed down by a large tripod camera, Karkaria travelled all across Iran on a journey that lasted over a year and took him to all the cities and ancient sites connected with Zoroastrianism. Making slow progress by donkey or on foot in pre-modern Iran, Karkaria halted at traditional caravanserais and experienced Iranian life at close quarters. This trip resulted in a travelogue titled *Iranbhoomi par Rakhad* (Rambles in Iran), clearly referencing the title of his war memoir, *Rangbhoomi par Rakhad.* It was published in 1925 by subscription. This travelogue is written in the same vein as his war memoir, humorous and self-deprecating, but is full of practical information and suggestions on how to navigate the mysteries of Iran. Every time he visited an ancient archaeological site, and there are many in Iran, Karkaria was exultant about the past glory of the Zoroastrians. Karkaria was hardly the first Parsi to imagine Persia as a fatherland which needed to be reclaimed by the Parsis. *Iranbhoomi par Rakhad* was just one of at least five Iran travelogues written by Parsis, which appeared in the interwar years. Karkaria, however, claims that his travels were the longest and his descriptions the most trustworthy.

Though the Bombay Pioneers were disbanded in 1933, Karkaria seems to have continued his association with the

Indian Army. When the Second World War commenced in 1939, it gave Karkaria, then in his mid-forties, another chance to participate in a world war. Although too old to see action, he seems to have been drafted into the war machine as a trainer. The only information I could find on his second stint in the army was that he was posted as a military instructor in Ranchi, one of the largest recruitment camps in India during the Second World War. Karkaria was promoted to major and stayed on at Ranchi even after the conclusion of the war, and was perhaps still associated with the Indian Army after the country gained independence in 1947.

Karkaria died after a short illness at the Military Hospital in Ranchi on 7 August 1949, at the age of fifty-four. A tiny obituary appeared in the eighth volume of *Parsee Prakash*, a community chronicle. During my two visits to Navsari, I tried to trace his family. The 1974 *Directory & Survey Report of the Parsis of Navsari* lists nearly fifty Karkarias, with most staying in the Mota Faliya neighbourhood. The Karkaria lane in Navsari was originally populated by the Karkaria clan, but none of the current residents had any memory going back to the 1940s.. Moreover, the few remaining Karkarias had not heard of Nariman Karkaria.

After his two books appeared in the 1920s, Karkaria does not seem to have published any more. In fact, he seems to have stepped away from the public eye. After his death in 1949, both he and his books were soon forgotten. Although the Parsi community continues to have a vibrant culture of necrology and hagiography, many Parsis have fallen through the chinks into oblivion. Karkaria is one of them.

When I discovered the war memoir of Nariman Merwanji Karkaria in 2012, the upcoming centenary of the First World War had generated great interest not just among global historians and scholars, but also among the general public. Conferences were being convened, new books were being published, old classics reissued, and a slew of commemorative events organized all over the world. There has been a major upswing in research related to the First World War, especially regarding the participation of Indians in the war, a subject which had hitherto been largely overlooked.

A few months after I came upon Karkaria's memoir in 2012, I encountered yet another war memoir written by an Indian. This was Captain (Dr) Gopal Gangadhar Limaye's *Sainyatil Athavani*, written in Marathi. Published in 1939, it is a record of his experiences from 1918 to 1921 with the Indian Army during the post-Great War military campaigns in the Middle East. Better educated and more observant than Karkaria, Limaye's account is more grounded in the political realities of the day but is equally gripping and deserves to be translated. A rigorous search might throw up a few more war memoirs or accounts in other Indian languages.

A note about the translation: it contains the entire text of *Rangbhoomi par Rakhad* in the same order as the Gujarati book, except for the chapter on Constantinople which has now been restored to its correct position. The original text is organized under a series of headings with no numbered chapters. I have divided the text into chapters and grouped them into five sections; the original subheadings have, however, been retained. The front matter and the list of subscribers have been omitted. Karkaria frequently spells out place names in English and I have used his preferred spellings. Numerous place names have changed since the 1920s, but I have retained the old names, including Kristania (Oslo), Tiflis (Tblisi) and Petrograd (St Petersburg). I have also retained the original years of historical events as mentioned by Karkaria.

I am thankful to the First Dastoor Meherjirana Library in Navsari, where I encountered the book again in 2013, for providing me with a working copy. My sister Meera conducted archival research on my behalf in London and also read and commented on the translation drafts. My friends, Kiran Subbaraman in Bengaluru and Animesh Mohapatra in New Delhi, provided valuable feedback. Amitav Ghosh readily agreed to my request to write a foreword to the book. To all of them, I am very grateful. And to Rahul Soni at HarperCollins for the love and care bestowed upon this book.

The publication of this English translation on the centenary of the publication of the original Gujarati book will, I hope, stimulate a greater interest in non-English sources for all aspects of the history of India, particularly military history.

Murali Ranganathan
Mulund, Mumbai
1 September 2020

Nariman Karkaria

BEFORE THE WAR

1

Decamping to China

It is common for great men to write accounts of their life. I certainly do not make any claims to greatness. Like my great-aunt used to say, it would be like blowing a tin whistle when a jazz orchestra was playing. But heck! I never could sit still. It seems I have been fated to roam the world and experience the worst kinds of hardships while traversing oceans, deserts, mountains and glaciers. From an early age, I have had the urge to travel. I could be in China one day, in England tomorrow, and perhaps tramping on sun-baked deserts the day after. You will read about all this as we go along, but right now my mind travels back to my turbulent childhood.

Childhood Days

I cannot stop myself from recalling those stormy days. Whenever I see young boys dutifully walking to school with their books, my mind travels back to my time at school. My antics during those wasted years caused my poor teacher to scream and shout at me. Just when it was time for a class to start, I would open a window and jump out to escape from the classroom. Either I would be tramping down the riverbank or I would be climbing up a tamarind tree and deriving pleasure by throwing stones at passing wayfarers. Those poor souls would holler, but it did not make a jot of a difference to me!

The following day, I would turn my attention to the schoolmaster. I would stick pins or needles into the seat of his chair; only when I heard his yelps as he sat down would I feel fulfilled. On the way back home, I would throw my books away and run screeching down the street, brandishing a stick in my hand. I would take pleasure in throwing dirt and stones into shops. When I recall these incidents, I hang my head in shame.

I had become habituated to leading a similar life at home. I was everybody's favourite and thoroughly pampered and would get whatever I demanded. I would not eat a morsel unless I was bribed with a few paise. If no money was forthcoming, I would create a racket. If I had to be given a haircut, my teacher, Edalji Kanga, would have to stand by with a rod, or else it was the barber who would get his hair cropped as I chased him right across the neighbourhood, yelling at the top of my voice. My poor mother and aunts would have to frequently apologize on my behalf.

Things continued in this stormy manner until I was twelve years old. One could say that I destroyed twelve years of my life. At the age of twelve, I was first taken on a trip to Mumbai and it was from then onwards that I began to change for the better. But as luck would have it, on this trip I became obsessed with travel. In Mumbai, I saw steamships and large ocean-going vessels for the first time and I was intimidated by their size. As a child, when I used to throw a tantrum, I would be threatened with being bundled off in one of those steamers, and that would sober me up.

The family began to hope that the situation would improve if I went through the Zoroastrian initiation ceremonies of navar and maratib. After I was initiated at the age of twelve, there was indeed a change in my behaviour. Unluckily for me, I was withdrawn from the regular school and set on course to become an andhiyaru, that is, to train towards becoming a priest. It was a new chapter in my life. I was, however, still quite tempestuous and often got into wrangles. I used to throw my weight around poor Parsi laymen, but they were rather tolerant of me and still thought of me as a child. But officiating in the agiary was becoming tiresome and it certainly did not sit well with my stormy nature. I always seemed to be a few steps ahead of my family's thoughts and practices. At this time, my twisted mind began to plot new adventures. A question used to keep popping up in my mind: Why had I not stepped out to experience the world? As if adding fat to the fire, a fashionable English-educated girl who was my friend taunted me about this shortcoming. I am not sure if it was my lucky day or not, but this was enough to fire me up. I decided that it was time to pack up my white priestly robes in a box and run away from the agiary. And once I had made up my mind, nothing could shake my resolve.

From Navsari to Mumbai

If one were to believe the stories told by Parsi shetias of old, the journey to the great country of China was a lot of fun. As for me, it was way out of the ordinary. The night of Saturday, the 10th of August 1910, was dark and black, and one of the most frightening nights of my life. It was on that night that I mustered the courage to set forth alone into the world at the age of sixteen. At about eight in the night, I slipped out of the house without letting anyone know. I just had a small bundle of clothes and a blanket with me. As I walked towards the railway station, which was at a little distance from the town, it began to drizzle lightly. The silence of the night was punctured by the roar of thunder and the flash of lightning. I was rather unnerved by the sound and light on those desolate roads and soon realized what I had got myself into. I was wondering where I should go. All kinds of thoughts began to race in my mind. I had all of fifty rupees in my pocket. I decided that my first destination would be Mumbai and I bought a third-class train ticket for this famous city.

When I reached Mumbai early next morning, the colourful city was awake and people were already bustling around. This energized me no end and I headed straight to the Pandey Dharamshala where I could stay for a few days. As a stranger to the ways of the city, I could feel people were staring at me as if I were an orangutan. It seemed to be perfectly obvious to everybody that I was a country yokel and not a resident of the city. It was the fashion in Mumbai to sit and browse a newspaper in the mornings. Although it was something I had never done, I thought it might be worthwhile to adopt this fashion, and bought a copy of *Jame Jamshed*. As luck would have it, my gaze fell on the advertisements while flipping the pages of the newspaper. The Rubatino Shipping Line Company's steamer *Capri* was scheduled to leave on Tuesday, the 13th of August 1910, for China. When I read this, a wild thought about going to China flashed in my mind. I had heard about the glories of that country frequently and I had often seen the sethias from China with their khobas, large red-coloured pagris. I would have been happy to exchange my white priestly pagri for this red one. I was wondering which liner to travel on. The Peninsular & Oriental was too fancy for a simpleton like me, who would be completely out of place on their ships. I therefore decided to go by the Rubatino Line's *Capri* and went to their office to make further inquiries. Luckily for me, there was a kindly old gentleman at the office who told me that the *Capri* was to leave at half past four on Tuesday afternoon. When I heard the passage would cost one hundred and seventy-five rupees, I was crushed. One hundred and seventy-five rupees? Oh God! I had only forty rupees left with me. Where was I to get the money? I racked my brain and finally decided to raise the money by selling the gold chain attached to my watch and the gold buttons on my jacket. For the first time in my life, I wandered from one Marwari shop to another, and finally, with a heavy heart and swollen eyes, sold those things which were dear to me. Using this money, I bought passage to Hong Kong, but I did not use my real name. I assumed the name of Nariman Nowroji Kanga. As I embarked on this thoughtless adventure, I wondered how my family would react to my disappearance. They loved me unconditionally and had always pampered me. They would never have permitted me to embark on such a long and arduous journey. In fact, I gave a false name at the passport office and to the steamer authorities just to give them the slip. This must have further saddened them when they got to know of it.

Let's Go to China!

It was about four in the evening. Just as the steamer began to puff out huge billows of smoke from its tall chimney, I reached the docks with a small bundle tucked under my armpit. It was chaos all around, with labourers running around frantically. To add to the noise, our steamer was emitting shrill whistles at short intervals as if it were saying its final goodbyes to the port of Mumbai. Never having experienced such levels of noise and activity before in my life, I was rather unnerved. When I saw the gangway leading up to the ship shaking violently, I involuntarily began to mutter a few prayers. There I was, all alone, with no one to see me off. Who was to strengthen my resolve? With a prayer on my lips, I walked up the steps and mounted what seemed like the back of a swaying elephant. In a few more minutes, the ship would leave the shores and face the huge waves of the ocean. If the ship were to continue to sway like this, it would be the end of the story for us in two minutes, wouldn't it? I can never forget the thoughts that passed through my head at that time. A couple of fair European damsels were waving their kerchiefs and blowing kisses to their friends on board. What was I to do when I saw them? In spite of being totally out of sorts and very frightened, I tried to amuse myself by waving my kerchief back at them.

My First Ocean Journey

The other passengers were busy unpacking their luggage, but what concern did I have with such tasks? I thought it better to stay inside my cabin. After a while, the bell for dinner was rung. But how was I to know it was the call for dinner? I was still inside my cabin when the waiter knocked on the door and informed me that the rest of the table was waiting for me. Only then did I realize that the bell was the call for dinner.

I entered the saloon dressed in the usual Parsi fashion, in a duglo and a topi. I had never before seen a saloon that was so well appointed and furnished in the European style. When I saw the assemblage of knives and forks and bottles of wine on the dining table, I broke into a cold sweat. Would I be able to survive this dining ritual? Though I did not even know in which hand to hold the fork and in which the knife, I was not particularly fazed. I just decided to do what the others on the table did. Soup was first served at the table, and like the others, I also sprinkled salt and pepper on it, though I did not then know what those little bottles contained. As it was an Italian liner, macaroni seemed to always be on the menu. The others seemed to like it very much and asked to be served again and again. They were stuffing the macaroni into their mouths and quaffing huge amounts of claret from the bottles which had been placed on the table. I thought it best to do as the others did and quickly drained a few glasses myself, although I did not particularly like the taste. When a bottle was empty, the waiter would immediately replace it with a full one. But how much can one drink? I was feeling rather uneasy. Even though I was not hungry, I continued to eat. At one stage, I could feel the vomit rising up towards my throat but I managed to suppress it. I somehow survived the entire dinner but had to immediately seek refuge in my cabin afterwards. Can you imagine my situation? I was feeling so sick that I wanted to jump off the ship into the ocean and return home. But was something like that written in my fate? The steamer *Capri* was chugging away furiously and it was not going to stop for someone like me. I was so out of sorts that I can barely remember the number of times I must have vomited that night. It all ended only after I quaffed a few inches of brandy and drifted away into sleep as I planned my future travels.

My Experiences on the Steamer

I slept like a log through the night. I was used to taking a shower immediately after I got up. After all, I was an andhiyaru, a Parsi priest who had been trained in the ritual of purification. There were quite a few passengers who were pacing up and down outside the bathroom early in the morning. Wearing an innocent look, I also joined the crowd. When the person inside emerged after a few minutes, I directly rushed into it without exchanging a glance with anybody else. A person from among those who were there before me rushed to block my way, but I managed to sneak in and bolted the door.

However, I did not particularly like the arrangements in the bathroom. For what seemed like half an hour, I hunted for a mug to take a bath. I tried to figure out how to use the bathtub. I had no clue how to take a bath in this bathroom. There was neither a bathing corner nor was there a bucket in which to fill water. When I opened one of the two taps attached to the front of the bathtub, it started sputtering out hot vapour which almost burnt my hand. I thought it would be prudent to leave this hell rather than attempt to take a bath.

Even though the ocean was as flat as a plate, many lady passengers with delicate constitutions often needed smelling salts in the morning. They would shut themselves up in their cabins and one could hear them frequently call out to the 'boy' for oranges and suchlike.

The days passed by rapidly. The steamer pressed on ahead after calling at Colombo, Penang and Singapore. One afternoon, it reduced its speed and crept ahead slowly as if it was afraid to collide with Hong Kong whose beautiful hillsides were now in full view. When the steamer entered Kowloon bay, it was boarded by Chinese porters. Their scrambling was a sight to behold. Since this was my first experience of visiting China, I was enthusiastically taking in everything. It was not as if one went to China every day.

A Miserable Sunday

However, this excitement lasted only for a short while. We had to now board steam launchers that would take us to Hong Kong, but I had no clue where to go once I reached land. There were thousands of Chinese people who were running around here and there. But what was I to ask them? As I did not know a word of Chinese, I thought it best to make my own way from the port. So, tucking my little bundle under my armpit, I began walking. There was no doubt all the pedestrians on the road were staring at me. If I stopped someone to ask a question, they would flash their teeth at me and walk away. And I would be left cursing them. What now? If one goes to an unknown country, this is bound to happen. I will never forget that miserable Sunday all my life. I did not know anything about the roads and the layout of the city, and wandered about aimlessly. I walked through many neighbourhoods populated by Chinese people.

I had started walking at about four in the evening. I had been climbing one hill after another but had no idea where I was headed. It was beginning to get dark and must have been getting to eight o'clock. It was just my misfortune that China was beginning to weigh me down. I had no more strength to keep walking. Haplessly, I sat on the steps of a house belonging to a Chinese. As I sank down, I burst into tears like a little boy. When I think of that moment, my eyes still moisten up. I confess that my situation was very pitiable at that time. All the excitement of having come to China had evaporated. But what could I do now? I somehow managed to pull myself together and set off walking again. As I walked towards an area that had many prosperous- looking bungalows, I suddenly let out a joyous whoop. Ah! What had I seen? It was an Indian watchman with a huge pagri. He was pacing up and down the road and chewing tobacco. What a delight! As I bounded towards him with tears of joy, he was taken aback for a moment. He first wondered what I wanted from him, but when I acquainted him with my situation, he began to nod his head in sympathy. I soon realized he was in no position to help me. I requested him to take me to the house of a Parsi gentleman, or else I would have to spend the night roughing it out in the open and perhaps die. He began pondering over what to do and finally led me up a winding road. We stopped outside a large bungalow, which he informed me belonged to Sir Hormusjee Modi. Having said this, he went away without any expectation of a baksheesh. Once he had gone, I entered the bungalow in style and asked to meet the elderly sethia. I was greeted by a Chinese man clad in a flowing dress, who had a long queue hanging down his back. He led me into a reception room that had been exquisitely decorated with Chinese furniture.

From Misery to Joy

I could not utter a word when I came face to face with the aged gentleman. I was so tired and traumatized that all I could do was burst into tears. He tried to comfort me and gave me a patient hearing. He was taken aback when he heard my entire story and tried to boost my morale in many ways. I began to think he was going to do only that, but I was mistaken. He had been so affected by my story that he felt I needed some reassurance. He offered me a large dose of brandy to strengthen my nerves and sent me off with two of his men to the office of Nusserwanjee Modi, which was located in the city. There I was offered a meal which, having starved through the day, tickled my Parsi taste buds. From there, I was taken by a man to the Parsi Club where arrangements had been made for my stay.

At the Parsi Club, I had to repeat my sad tale to its caretaker, the Dustoorjee Saheb, who also took it upon himself to advise me. It was well past midnight when, after having suffered all through the day, I lay down on a mattress and brought the curtain down on a miserable Sunday. When I woke up the next morning, I discovered that the adventures of the 'misguided runaway' were being hotly discussed by everyone there. Everyone was keen to catch a glimpse of me to see what kind of person would do such a deed. Some of them sympathized with me, while others made fun of me. And as if this was not enough, the Hong Kong correspondent of *Jame Jamshed* took it upon himself to convey the news of my arrival in China to India. This is what was published in the newspaper:

PARSI BOY LOST IN HONG KONG

In his letter of the 15th of September, our Hong Kong correspondent writes that: having heard the names of the rich businessmen of China, and fascinated by travel on an ocean-going steamer, and hoping to partake of the riches of China, a fifteen-year-old Parsi schoolboy has arrived in Hong Kong on board the steamer *Capri*. As the boy is rather smart, he has been able to muster the courage to make this journey alone. It seems he has been taken in by rumours that one can get a job on landing in Hong Kong. Having heard the name of Sir Hormusjee Modi, he tried to reach his residence after alighting from the steamer. However, somebody had the sense to direct him to the offices of Nusserwanjee Modi & Co. The entire Parsi community has been taken aback by his derring-do and the employment prospects of such a young boy have been the topic of discussion. However, Mr Jamshedjee Jeejeebhoy of Jeejeebhoy & Co. deserves to be congratulated for having offered him a job in their new store on Hollywood Road in spite of there being really no requirement. I take this opportunity through the columns of your newspaper to warn those who come or intend to come to Hong Kong without any assured employment or proper references that the business prospects and reputation of China are no longer what they used to be and exist only in name.

– *Jame Jamshed*, 4 October 1910

2
Life in China

Would anybody take up a job at a salary of fifteen rupees a month after having travelled thousands of miles? Sheer stupidity, some might say. But what did you expect? Such were my circumstances in those days. Is there any point in worrying too much? I considered myself fortunate that my spirits were as buoyant as ever in spite of having experienced numerous hardships. Was it possible to quickly make a fortune in a strange country? During those terrible days, even a job that paid fifteen rupees a month was a saving grace. I was not in the least ashamed to do such a low-paying job and began to work earnestly at the store on Hollywood Road. Those businessmen did need to hire someone, unlike what the correspondent of *Jame Jamshed* had to say; or else why would they hire me?

I had to continue working as usual even on important days such as Pateti, which passed by without any fanfare. There was no fuss about wearing crisply ironed white clothes suitable for an andhiyaru and no gazing at fair Parsi ladies in their resplendent clothes. The whole day passed by listlessly without event.

In this manner, each day would disappear into the next. From opening the doors at six in the morning until it shut down at nine in the night, I spent the whole day at the store. After having worked the whole day, I had to spend two hours learning at the night school. How could an impetuous lad like me tolerate this prison-like schedule? It was a tough pill to swallow, but what could I do except cry into my pillow every night? However, even this miserable period did not last for many months. When arduous journeys had been written in my fate, I could hardly be expected to stand behind a counter for long. There were signs that I might lose my job when the bosses merged two of their stores into one. As the staff was surplus and there was less work to do, I inevitably got into mischief. This did not go down well with the bosses, who began to keep a close eye on me. It felt like the black clouds of Hong Kong were circling me. As the old proverb goes, even a sneeze merited a reprimand, and ultimately I was even branded a thief. I soon realized this place was not for me. After a stint of eleven months, the first phase of my journey came to an end, and I left the Parsi Club with the same meagre belongings I had come with.

From Hong Kong to Peking

Hong Kong no longer appealed to me. While wasting an hour or so packing my little bundle of clothes, I decided to move on. At that point, it suddenly occurred to me that I should pay a visit to mainland China. Not long after that, on the 8th of June, I found myself on Butterfield & Swire's steamship, *Hui Chow*, as it made its way across the ocean. The steamer was resounding with the conversation of Chinese passengers. I could now bandy around a few words of Chinese myself; perhaps they thought I was some sort of Chinese raja? They gave me perplexed stares. My pockets were practically empty and I had to travel on the deck, which was a level lower than third class. But I was not ashamed of my situation. There must be very few people who have been fortunate enough to travel together with Chinese people. You could lounge wherever you wanted and eat whenever you were hungry without bothering about an evening dress for dinner. And there was no cabin or luggage to worry about. You could have great fun lounging on the deck and taking in the beautiful sights of the Hong Kong harbour. There are few other harbours in the world which look as beautiful from the ocean as Hong Kong does. You could forget all your worries as you gazed at it. It was my good luck that the ocean was very calm that day and it was as if the ship was gliding smoothly on it. But soon enough, the silence was punctured by the sound of an instrument being played by one of the passengers. Only someone with a punctured eardrum could sit in front of such an instrument. Even our dear nankhatai bands are not a patch on it.

Anchor at Midnight

It was very hot on the 10th of June when the ship dropped anchor in complete silence near Shanghai, on the famous Yangtze-Sinkiang river, at about three o'clock at night when we were in deep slumber. At dawn, Chinese workers began to bustle around and haul the anchor back into the ship. At quarter to seven, the steamship's engines began to drone again and we soon set off up the Huangpu river. There is a place called Wusong upstream where the river is very shallow. As the ships prefer to cross the bar at daylight, they anchor overnight before moving up further. The famous river Yangtze-Sinkiang (what a mouthful!) is said to be the biggest river in all of Asia and Europe. It is about 3,328 miles long and drains about 900,000 square miles. It is quite a challenge for the steamers to navigate it. The Huangpu River meets the Yangtze at its mouth. After halting at Shanghai, the *Hui Chow* ploughed on further and called at Tsing Tao, Chi Koo and Dalniy ports. It was at Tsing Tao (then known as Kiaow Chou) that the Germans put up a valiant response to an attack by the Japanese during the Great War. Under the care of the Germans, Tsing Tao, my favourite city, has blossomed into a beautiful place and is lacking for nothing. On the way, one can spend a couple of hours at Chi Koo to see the famed silk manufacturing workshops. At Dalniy (or Dalian), now controlled by Japan, it feels like one is strolling in a Japanese city. One can also see the factory of the South Manchuria Railway at Dalniy. One should also not miss the famous Nihon Bridge at Dalniy, which is still adorned with ancient carvings. After a voyage of eight days, the ship left the China Sea and entered the inner waters of the Bohai Sea where our journey terminated at Tientsin. Trains were waiting to take the passengers to all corners of China. If one wanted to go to the Chinese capital Peking, the Tientsin–Peking railway line would take you there in four hours. One train leaves in the morning and there is one more in the evening. If one has a few hours to spare, Tientsin is worth wandering around. The European-style houses of the Legations and the hustle-bustle of military activities are a sight worth seeing. There are a couple of Zoroastrian shops in Tientsin where, on most days, one can enjoy Parsi food. The Parsis in China are quite welcoming. I satiated myself by having my morning meal at the premises of Messrs H. Viccajee before turning towards the sprawling Tientsin station at three in the afternoon. What a terrible sight! The chaos of the place surpassed even our noxious fish markets. Baby-footed Chinese women were running around pell-mell in every direction, some with bundles of hay, and others with baskets of foul-smelling stuff.

The Chinese Capital, Peking

If one ever has to travel on the Chinese railways, you should never venture below the first class. The third-class carriages are like our goods wagons: no seats, no nothing! You can squat anywhere you want on the floor. The second class has rows of little seats like in our tramcars. And sometimes, there is a table between two rows that face each other. All those fat Chinese people with big paunches can barely squeeze themselves in; and having done that, they can hardly move an inch. They have to sit in the same position all through the journey. It is certainly worth blowing five dollars on a first-class ticket. At least one can gaze at the passing countryside with its greenery and farms. I saw ponytailed Chinese labourers driving ploughs pulled by Chinese mules. It was fun to see the labourers lashing the mules with long whips. The mules were so decrepit that it seemed they might die in a day or two.

As I took in the passing scenery, our train chugged into Peking station at about half past seven in the evening. It was not as if a reception party was waiting for me at the station. I did not have to waste any time looking out for anybody and strode out of the station, lifting my luggage myself. As I was a complete stranger to the city, I wondered which route to take in order to reach my destination. After wandering up and down wrong roads a few times, I reached the British Legation, where I was to start my new job, a little after eight at night. I had managed to advance a step in this second job, and instead of fifteen rupees a month, I would be paid fifty rupees at the European firm of William Forbes & Co. Since their clients included the British Army, I would occasionally get into minor arguments with the Tommies, otherwise this job was hardly stressful. As the management of the firm in Peking was handled by a Parsi, I had a lot of freedom to roam around town. Even though there were then only six Parsis in Peking, they were at daggers drawn! All six of them were extremely crabby, and one had to be mindful about encountering them while walking around the city.

Let's See China

Having come all the way to Peking, one might as well have a look around. As the capital city of the great land of China, it has got quite a reputation. But one should not be readily taken in by it. One might end up being disappointed if one expressly made a trip to Peking to take in the sights. If you intend to make a tour of its streets, you had better empty a bottle of scent into your handkerchief so that you can mask any other smell.

Peking has been carved into two areas in which the Chinese and the foreigners stay separately. The foreigners stay in an area commonly referred to as the 'Town'. After the fighting during the Boxer Uprising of 1900, the population of foreigners in Peking increased rapidly. For their safety, units of the British, French, German, American, Russian, Japanese, Belgian, Italian and Spanish armies are maintained in the respective Legations, and their expenses are debited to the revenues of the poor Chinese government. If there is even a hint of a disturbance among the Chinese, all the foreign businessmen are herded into their respective Legations. The streets of the Town are lined with the huge stores and banks of the foreign businessmen. The Chinese part of the city, which is known as 'Tienanmen', contains innumerable shops of Chinese businessmen. Wherever you go, you can see Chinese shopkeepers, Chinese houses, Chinese shops, and the roads are full of Chinese men with long ponytails. Chinese, Chinese, and only Chinese! If you threw your weight around in this part of town, you might as well be dead. No appeal, no trial! You had better be careful.

Let us now pop into a few of these shops. The most exciting ones are those that sell a range of cooked food. The most popular item seems to be boiled egg. Can you imagine what it is like? It is deadly black in colour, and if you were to hold it to your nose, you might swoon! Hope you have some cologne water on hand. And if you take it up to your ears, you can hear a sound! The Chinese consider this kind of hard, black and smelly egg to be a delectable treat. They consider this egg to be fully ripe and perfect to eat, while they believe fresh eggs are too raw. Similarly, there are many other kinds of cooked preparations on display, but what takes things to another level are dried rats. The dried rats are slit into two all the way up to the heads and are hung on display. You will be treated to an exhibition of different animals and birds: owls, geese, turtles, pigs and fish, all fried and dried. All you have to do is eat. The Chinese do not miss out on eating anything. If you have a Chinese cook in your house, you had better be very careful. Check what he has brought from the market before he cooks it, or else you will have no clue as to what you have been fed. Once our Chinese cook eagerly served us a dish for dinner. We gobbled it up without bothering to check what it was. In fact, it was so tasty that we asked for a second helping. It was only when we began to praise his cooking skills that he let it slip out that the frogs in this part of China were very tasty. What the hell! My eating companion lost his cool when he heard this. We spent the whole night imagining those accursed frogs jumping up to our throats from our stomachs before slipping back in. What were we to do now? It was best to keep quiet, or else our Chinese cook would disappear without a trace the next morning.

Parsi ladies seem to believe that there is no other place in the world as advanced as China, and they extol the virtues of Chinese cloth to the skies. All this is because of the good quality of Chinese cloth. If ever the word 'China' was mentioned, my poor dear mother would ardently hope and exclaim that I grew up to be as smart as the Chinese. But they do not know the current condition of China. It is indeed true that China can claim to be the oldest kingdom in the world. Its history dates back to nearly

4,500 years, or about 2,700 years BC, since the first Chinese emperor, Hwangti, established his kingdom. In spite of such a long tradition, education is in short supply. However, at the same time, the Chinese are certainly very industrious.

The Famous Wall of China

The evidence of the existence of this wall goes back to 2,100 years, that is, to the reign of the Chinese emperor Shi Huang. The Chinese were being attacked incessantly by the Tartars. To prevent these everyday attacks, the emperor decided to fortify the borders of his kingdom, but this was not a task that could be done at the snap of a finger. If the entire northern boundary had to be fortified, it was estimated that the wall would stretch to about 1,500 miles. What? A wall stretching 1,500 miles? But then it was the king who had issued the order, so work on building the wall commenced. Hundreds of labourers were kidnapped and made to forcibly work on the site. Besides, some of them found themselves buried inside the walls along with the huge stones and lime mortar. Well, at least it is still famous, and when visitors come face to face with the wall, they actually let out screams of shock and disbelief as if a little mouse has crept into their mouths. The skill evident in the construction makes them bob their heads in appreciation. This is no ordinary wall. Six horsemen can ride in parallel on the top of the wall. In the mornings, groups of cyclists can be seen having fun riding on top of the wall, and walkers like me can take in the sights of the city while twirling their swagger sticks. Handsome benches have been placed at intervals for their comfort, and even beautiful ladies do not hesitate to make use of them. There is also a lot of greenery on top. What else can you see on the wall? Pagodas, forty feet tall, have been erected at regular intervals. You can see far into the distance from the tops of these pagodas. The wall itself is fairly high, about twenty to thirty feet from the ground. And it is about twelve feet broad. Starting at Shanhaiguan, the wall enters Peking, and after encircling the city, it goes on all the way beyond Manchuria, before it finally ends at Kowkon to the west of Suchaoni in Mongolia. If the Chinese people ever get up to any kind of mischief, you can be sure that the German cannons atop the wall will start firing. The Germans have appropriated a part of the wall and installed cannons on it, while the American troops have also set up camp on it. What an irony!

Chinese Death Rituals

Have you ever heard a Chinese pray? If you have not, accompany me. As I am an andhiyaru myself, I can make similar sounds. Chinese priests are not very different from our Parsi dustoors. If there has been a death in any house, it is quite an experience to hear these priests praying all through the night. The Chinese keep the corpse for three days in their house before setting off on the final journey. In earlier times, the corpse used to be preserved for many more days. There is no difference between a Chinese marriage and a Chinese funeral; both processions involve music. The persona of their religious leaders is a sight to behold—a flat hat of white satin and long flowing white garments. Of course, a ponytail hangs down their backs. Or else how can they conduct the final rituals? If the rituals are not properly conducted, the dead might come back as ghosts to harass the living. The Chinese are extremely superstitious about rituals concerning the dead. Compared to them, our Parsis seem to be slightly better off. The Chinese are even afraid to take a corpse out of the house. If it is taken out through the main door, then the ghost will learn how to enter the house. Therefore, so as to deceive the ghost, the body is lowered down to the road from an opening in the upper floor. A special platform is erected for this purpose. About eight to ten labourers are needed to ensure that the coffin containing the body is lowered properly. Once the body is safely out of the house, they heave a sigh of relief, confident that the ghost has been well and truly deceived. The body is then escorted in a procession headed by a priest, with a band playing musical instruments. It is followed by a person holding a yoke on his shoulder, from which hang panniers containing utensils. How else will the dead person cook?

The Chinese lamas hold the highest position among the religious orders and enjoy the same prestige as our Parsi dustoors. There are many such lamas in the Lama Temple at Peking. They have the hair on their head shaved off at childhood. Many illiterate women take vows to send their sons into the lama order. In fulfilment of such vows, many unfortunate children have their heads tonsured at an early age and they are never allowed to grow their hair again. The lamas are said to be very influential. There are about a thousand bald-headed lamas in the Lama Temple at Peking, of whom quite a few are women and children.

The Famous Lama Temple at Peking

Let us examine the present condition of this temple. It is in a dilapidated state. The situation is so precarious that it might collapse today or tomorrow. From what survives, one can, however, make out that it must have been very prosperous in earlier times. It seems that about ten temples have been brought together to form this large temple. Originally they must have been temples dedicated to individual gods. The roofs taper upwards, and the structure has been built in the form of a boat in the ancient Chinese architectural style. Statues of Buddhist gods have been arranged at different levels, according to their relative importance, as if in an exhibition. There must be over 1,500 of these statues. If you wish to examine each of them individually, you might as well fortify yourself with some munchies. And if you hire a guide, he will rattle off the names of each of these statues for you. You could arm yourself with a 1,000-page notebook to jot down the names.

The festivities of these lamas are an impressive sight. When these so-called dustoors sit down for their rituals, they don a hat which is about a yard high and a dress which reaches below their ankles. The head lama occupies his seat on a cushion placed in the centre and the other lamas seat themselves around him. The festivities start with the burning of various kinds of incense in a large burner. They certainly do not put in any eggs or anything of that sort.

Hold on! Slowly, if you please! If you race up these stairs, you might just topple the whole thing over and be crushed under a pile of stones. We are on our way up to the bell tower to see what is supposed to be the biggest bell in China. Before climbing up the stairs, you might as well insure your life and ensure the future of your children. A part of the bell has long since fallen off and what remains is in so precarious a condition that it might bring everything down one of these days. The history of the Chinese emperors is carved on the inner and outer surfaces of this bell. It is also considered to be the oldest bell. It was, however, intended to be used for a very different purpose. The bell used to be rung when the temple was under threat, but it has not been rung in a very long time. I forgot to mention, there is also a Parsi temple within this Lama Temple. Well, some might say I am bluffing, but it is true. A very large picture in the temple caught my attention. The images which had been painted on it closely match those of heaven and hell that can be seen in the *Arda Viraf Nama*. Below the images are some lines of text written in Sanskrit. Unfortunately, its condition has deteriorated to such an extent that not a single letter can be read. But if someone actually wants to see heaven, you can come with me to the Temple of Heaven.

Temple of Heaven

When you visit the Temple of Heaven, you can see specimens of the strangest things in the world! And if you go to the West, all you can do is drink champagne and have fun. Three things are considered to be the most important in the Chinese religion: heaven, earth and humans, that is, man. Although the Chinese emperor falls in the third category, he is worshipped as a divine being. However, in the present times, when there is no religion, where is the question of worshipping the emperor?

If you enter the Temple of Heaven, it is almost as if you have reached heaven! All you have to do is climb the steep steps that lead up to it. As the temple is located at a little distance from the town, one has to go there by donkey. In Peking, there are donkeys, donkeys, and more donkeys! On every road, Chinese syces stand in readiness with their donkeys which have been saddled like horses. All you have to do is sit on them. When our dear Chinese sit on these donkeys, it is quite a sight to behold. And these donkeys are so quick-paced that you will reach your destination after a ride of two or three hours with a rather sore back. But don't you have to undergo a little hardship to reach heaven? And indeed, the temple, which is the best place to see in Peking, is like heaven. There are galleries upon galleries of beautiful Chinese art in the temple. The gallery at the lowest level is about 200 feet long, while the one at the top is said to be about 90 to 100 feet long. Though it is quite an effort to see this place, it is certainly worth it. There is a big hall where the Chinese emperor performs his religious rituals. He believes his status is just below that of heaven.

The place where the emperor performs his rituals contains a stone structure with nine levels that are supposed to represent the nine heavens. There are stairs that lead all the way to the top. He ascends these stairs on his knees and prostrates full length at each level. He is then considered to be the representative of heaven. It is as if the Chinese have recreated heaven on earth. In earlier times, only the emperor could worship in this temple, and this ascent to heaven would happen during the winters when people from all over China would come to Peking to have a glimpse of the Temple of Heaven.

The Sorry State of Chinese Women in Peking

If you have never ever seen a Chinese woman, then Peking is the place to do so. Let me show you a few Chinese women from the capital city of Peking. These ladies must have committed a variety of sins in their previous lives for which they have been punished in this life with no feet. To be sure, they do have feet, but it is considered fashionable to reduce them in size. Even in our country, there are many ladies with feet as big as shovels who feel extremely sorry for themselves. Poor things! But the craze for tiny feet in Peking is such that Chinese women, be they rich or poor, have their feet bound from childhood. It is done in a very pitiless manner; except for the big toe, the other toes are bound inwards into the base of the feet. How does it matter if pus dribbles out of the one toe which is free? The feet are then enclosed in tight boots. How are they to grow? The tinier the feet, the more fashionable it is considered. But the real fun starts when these ladies grow old. A man has to be appointed to take care of them. When they have to step out of the house, the man hoists them on his shoulders just like a Parsi grandfather hoists his granddaughter.

But this is not where the story ends. These women are at real risk when a house is on fire because they cannot run down the stairs and get out of the house fast enough. Because of this, many of them have been burnt to death. And our dear Chinese are so kind that, instead of helping them, they stand by laughing and enjoying the show. And as if this is not enough, the scoundrels use this opportunity to run away with anything valuable from the burning house, including some of those beautiful young ladies with little feet who are then sold in the neighbouring town at high prices. No appeal, no justice, no nothing! The pursuit of fashion leads to unintended consequences.

The Chinese Bun

Another fashion that draws our attention is the practice among Chinese women of tying their hair in a bun. It is so impressive that even our Parsi ladies would appreciate it. If a Parsi lass of eighteen ever twirled the hair on her forehead, an old family retainer would rush to envelop her in a shawl. On the other hand, these Chinese ladies take a minimum of three hours to comb their hair and form it into a bun. It is as if they are in competition with each other. If you see five Chinese ladies fanning themselves as they stroll down the road, you will notice that each of them has styled her hair differently. Not only is the hair arranged in different patterns, but they also wind a strip of black cloth around it, which is supposed to enhance their beauty by a few degrees. But if you look at their faces, you will immediately forget about their hair. What do I call it? Is it a powder, a colour, or chalk which these Manchurian ladies apply on their faces? God has endowed them with a rosy beauty, but these unfortunate souls slather so much colour on their faces they can hardly be recognized. Their true beauty is hidden, but they could not give a damn about it. They have to keep up with the prevailing trends in fashion, be it while sitting, sleeping or even sneezing. Fashion, fashion, and more fashion!

Well, let's not get involved with them too much because we are here to work and earn money. However, I was again beginning to get restless. Do you know why? By this time, I had saved enough money that I could hear the jingling of coins in my pocket.

Retreat from China

Fate is a strange thing! It was time to move on again. One day I was in the great land of China, and the next I found myself in Hindustan. Dame Fortune was toying with me. There I was in the middle of all the action, and suddenly I am back to drinking toddy in Navsari. I had no second thoughts after it occurred to me to come back to India. It did not take me too long to act on my thoughts. And there I was, walking down Mota Falia to get a drink of toddy. Having come back from a voyage to China, I was considered a hero! My mother was relieved to see me again and the neighbours were proud of me. Whenever I walked around, people would stare and point at me as if I was a clown in a ridiculous hat. Damsels would flash admiring smiles at me. It was all I could desire.

However, it has never been in my fate to stay at home. Having had a taste of the outside world, I was never going to be happy in Navsari. I was admittedly a sahib in China, but back home, I had reverted to being a black man. But I was not bothered about such stuff. Now that it was getting on six months, ten months, even twelve months, I was, as the Tommies would say, 'Fed up!' of this black town. China had not been particularly welcoming the first time around, but was that reason enough to admit defeat? No!

China also had its redeeming features. But was it worth trusting the place? Wondering what was in store for me, I decided to make a second trip to China. Once I decided to do something, nothing could make me change my decision. I decided to go via Calcutta this time. As this was my third visit to Calcutta, it was not a strange city for me. And anyway, I was now a seasoned traveller. What was there to be afraid of?

3

Off to the War

With each passing day, I was putting on more sinews on my chest. I had no idea what my fate had in store for me and wondered what travel plans God had made for me. For now, I boarded the steamship *Kuk Sang* which was to leave on the 20th of February at about seven in the evening. It was like jumping into the sea again.

But what is all this sound and noise? It is a fight, but not an ordinary one where women scream and pull out each other's hair. This is a ruinous battle: fighting in the air, fighting on land, fighting at sea, fighting everywhere. My dear Parsis in Hong Kong and Shanghai seemed to have got into fighting mode. They would beat their chests and proudly proclaim themselves volunteers. I was a little taken aback by this new turn in the world's affairs. I had no idea what it meant to be a volunteer in the war! Someone would mention he was on guard duty the whole night without any food or water, while another would claim he had to attend a parade early in the morning. On my very first day in China, I realized that an innocent person like me should have nothing to do with such military affairs. I thought it best to proceed to Peking, which was my ultimate destination. But things were twice as bad there. It was like jumping from the frying pan into the fire! Practically everyone was talking about the war. Wherever I went, people would comment that a young man like me should be on the battlefield. And then there were others who advised me otherwise. As a result, I was in a quandary about what I should be doing. After all, martial Iranian blood was coursing through my veins. How long could I let the situation drift? It was time to jump into the battlefield and disembowel a German or two!

Expression of Martial Enthusiasm Within Me

Had I not read quite a few tales of battles in the *Burjornama*? Would it not have had any effect on me? I just had to fight, and fight I would. And on the way to the war, I would be able to see towns nestling in the icy mountains of Siberia and Russia. I was looking forward to it, but a friend mentioned that it was not a big deal: 'Siberia and Russia are about as distant from Peking as Navsari is from Mumbai and it is very easy to get there.' This outlandish comparison turned out to be true, but only after I had practically reached my final destination: London. A Parsi warned me about the cold in Siberia; it was so intense that your legs would freeze and would have to be cut off. Another Parsi told me that I had to always strap a heater around my waist to keep myself warm, while a third said that I would have to stitch a thick lining inside my boots. I was scared when I heard them. I was, after all, a village bumpkin who could be frightened very easily. But what was to be done?

My Last Parsi Meal in the Chinese Capital

With no little effort, I tried to equip myself to combat the cold of the North Pole. The astrologer had divined the date of 17th of November as the most appropriate for my departure. I had my last Parsi meal at the premises of Messrs H. Viccajee & Co. that evening; and a sumptuous one it was, accompanied by champagne. At about nine o'clock at night, a large group of Zoroastrians accompanied me to the Peking railway station. It was as if the train was restlessly waiting just for us. We first went to the dining car where I bought everybody a round of drinks, just to wet their throats. This was supposed to be a safeguard against the cold winds of Siberia, instead it left me poorer by ten dollars before I even started my journey. But at least I was heartily toasted by my friends. Was going to Russia as easy as sucking on a lollipop?

Just about then, the train let out a shrieking whistle. My friends scrambled out of the dining car and screamed out their final goodbyes in Parsi fashion as the train snaked its way into the dark. Ah! I was on my way. But if you intend to travel from Peking to Russia, you had better not forget to get yourself a 'passport' in the Russian language from the Russian representative at Peking, as you are not going to meet anybody who knows English during your entire journey. And you better travel by the Siberian 'through mail', or else you might never reach your destination. There are three trains every week from the Chinese capital, which travel to Siberia. There is one on Monday night, the 'through express' on Wednesday at 9.45, and the third on Friday night. You will have to fork out 198 roubles for the first-class fare from Peking to St Petersburg, while a second-class seat will set you back by 133 roubles. This was when a rouble was worth two rupees. And the fare from Petrograd to New Castle, including the steamer and the train, is 228 roubles for the first class and 157 for the second class. I have no idea how much the fare has increased to now. There is no point in worrying about the fare since you can travel only if you have the money. It is not as if your outlay is limited to the fare. You also have to pay for your food and drink. And how much do you think they cost? A cup of coffee in the dining car will set you back by three-quarters of a rupee. They do not seem to be troubled by any sense of guilt at these outrageous prices. And it is not as if there are vendors who are walking the carriages shouting, 'Tea! Tea!' You are not going to see any such thing on a Chinese train. It is all rather quiet there. The train left Peking at ten in the night and it reached Mukden at 8.30 p.m. the next night. At Mukden, we said goodbye to the Chinese rattleboxes and boarded the comfortable Japanese train.

The Luxuries of Japanese Train Travel

Our dear dwarf Japanese have done wonders with their trains. Indian trains are not a patch on them. Even their second-class carriages are like saloons fit for a king. The sleeping arrangements are extremely comfortable. An attendant comes in to make your bed at nightfall. The mattresses are soft enough to sink in, while the blankets are such that you would not feel like getting out of them. If they can lay out a Japanese nightdress for you to sleep in, would they forget to give you a towel and soap to wash your face when you get up? All of this is arranged by your bedstead. If you need something in the middle of the night, you can press an electric button installed near your bed without getting up. You will be promptly attended to by a waiter who is specially assigned to the carriage. Do you think all this comes for free? For a night's journey from Mukden to Changchun, one would have to pay eight fen, that is, a mere eighteen rupees. Wonder what the rate is now!

The entire intelligence of the short-statured Japanese seems to be concentrated in their bald heads. The seats in the carriages are so arranged that three people can sit in one row. As they have installed hand rests between each seat, one cannot stretch out in these seats even if the carriage is empty. How else would people pay so much money for their sleeper carriages? Having left Mukden in the night, the train reached Changchun station at 6.30 in the morning. The Russian express train was waiting for us at Changchun. The Russian and Japanese stations have been built at a short distance from each other, both staffed by personnel from the respective countries. The Siberian Mail, which would take us to Harbin via Shuangchengzhen, would depart after a halt of two hours.

The Cavernous Harbin Railway Station

It takes just seven hours to traverse the distance between Changchun and Harbin. It was only four in the morning when our train entered the cavernous railway station of Harbin. As the train pulled into the station, the scramble of the huge Russian porters was a sight worth seeing. They quickly get into the train, unload your luggage and deposit it in the storeroom. When I first saw them, I was rather taken aback and wondered where they were taking my luggage. As they were all Russian, they did not understand a word of English. As I ran shouting after them, trying to figure things out, a small audience gathered to watch the show. But did I have a choice? One routinely faced such problems in strange lands. Finally things were clarified and I was assured that I did not have to worry about my luggage. All I had to do was remember the badge number of the porter. He was responsible for my luggage and would load it back on the train in which I was scheduled to depart. I did not have to bother about it any more.

Why should I lie? The minute I entered Siberia, I forgot all my worries and troubles. The station at Harbin was rather welcoming and the congenial Russian beauties were a sight for sore eyes. They were as well built as the women from Kabul. They could easily dispatch any unwelcome admirer, such as those one sees on the streets of Mumbai, with just a slap.

Comfort Women Offered by the Railways

The hustle-bustle at Harbin railway station reminded me of the Grant Road station in Mumbai. Towards evening, little schoolgirls returning home from school presented a pleasing sight. With a slate and books in their hand, these beautiful little ones with rosy red cheeks would grab the attention of the passing traveller. Running here and there, they flashed coy stares with their little eyes. All of them had their hair cut in the latest fashion, their locks cascading in graduated lengths over their cheeks, and as they kept bobbing their heads, it was as if they were taking part in a beauty pageant.

There were more sights waiting for me outside Harbin station. Since my train was scheduled to depart at one in the night, I thought I might as well stroll into the town and take in the sights. As I walked down the main street, I was hoping to see something interesting and new—and I was not disappointed. The road was lined with huge restaurants. I suddenly felt like popping into a shop selling Russian sweets. When I looked into the shop, I could see that the shelves were lined with a variety of attractive sweets. There were quite a few customers and I thought I might also buy something to eat. With one hand stuffed into my trouser pockets, I confidently walked into the shop. To my surprise, I was immediately greeted by two Russian girls who welcomed me with sparkling smiles. I was a little flustered and wondered what exactly they wanted from me. I later discovered it is the practice in all the shops at Harbin to hire female attendants to wait on their customers. Only God knew what they were saying in Russian as they kept flashing smiles at me. I walked in nonchalantly as

I smiled back. Unluckily, my wallet had to take a big hit. Every item had a price tag affixed to it. It was quite a contrast to our fish markets; there was no need to waste any energy haggling about the prices. You would just have to silently point out the item you wanted as if you were dumb and pay the price.

I was now beginning to feel a little peckish. I walked into Hotel Grand, which was right opposite the station. Although the hotel was indeed grand, the food served there did not appeal to my taste. It was as if I had donated my money to charity. As it was getting darker, I returned to the station and decided to rest awhile in the waiting room. But when I entered it, all my tiredness and sleep suddenly vanished. It was brightly lit and decorated as if it were a garden party. A variety of plants in beautiful Chinese pots dotted the room, and colourful candles were placed on the tables. The chandeliers transformed the room into a paradise fit for angels. You could just sink into the plush sofas, and if you felt like it, even catch a few winks. As there was a refreshment room adjoining the waiting room, I thought I might as well have a cup of coffee. When I entered the room, it was as if all eyes were on me, wondering who I was. I just ignored the stares and settled into a sofa and ordered a coffee. Even before the coffee arrived, the situation took a rather unexpected turn. A gaudily made-up girl came and sat down next to me and began making eyes at me. While I was trying to figure out what this meant, the girl sidled up to me and began talking to me as if we had known each other for ages. For the sake of courtesy, I ordered a cup of coffee for her. Only later did I find out from the Chinese man in the refreshment room that these girls are available in every station to keep passengers company. And indeed they were! In every station, I saw similar farces being enacted.

Paper Notes for Copper Coins

At about 1.15 in the night, the postal train I had to board puffed into Harbin station. The porter who had earlier taken away my luggage came back to deposit it in the train. After he confirmed that everything was 'All correct, sir!', you would have to pay him the rather exorbitant charges for his services. What do you think they were? You would have to pay ten kopeks for each piece of luggage, irrespective of its size. And as if this much money were not enough, you could delight him by tipping him ten kopeks for his services, and he would salute you as many times as you wanted.

As Russian currency was current from Harbin onwards, one would no longer have to bother about counting copper coins and hauling them around. But my first discovery of this simple system was a little embarrassing. When I'd had a cup of coffee at Harbin station the previous night, I had paid with a sparkling silver rouble. In return I'd got little paper stamps with ten kopeks written on them. I was not particularly impressed and began arguing with the cashier. While he tried to explain the matter to me in his non-existent English, I accused him of being a thief in the Russian I had learnt at Navsari: 'When I gave you a sparkling coin, how dare you give me postage stamps in return? I don't intend to post any letters, so give my change in real money.' As usual, an audience quickly gathered around us. Ultimately, I became the laughing stock when I finally realized that these were not postage stamps, but paper notes of very small denomination. I offered a few words of apology and quietly backtracked amidst much laughter. This was when I realized one need not be saddled by the weight of coins in this country. You could stuff as many notes, ranging from five kopeks to hundred kopeks in your pocket, and they would not make a sound.

Water Kettles at Railway Stations

Since I was travelling in a post train, there was no dining car attached to it. And I did not particularly miss it during the night. Having left Harbin at night, we reached the capacious Manchuria station at about six in the morning, where I had to change trains. I had to go through the whole rigmarole of unloading my luggage. I went around looking for a cup of tea since it is available only at the larger stations. However, at every station, one can spot a little hut where a kettle of boiling water is always kept ready. Passengers can fill their own teapots with this boiling water and make themselves a hot cup of tea. When the train pulls into the station, one can see passengers running towards the hut to get their kettles filled. Why would anyone say no to something available for free? You do not have to pay a single paisa for this service. If you plan to travel in these parts, you had better bring along a teapot. Don't forget tea and sugar either!

4
Through Siberia to Russia

From Manchuria station, a separate line goes towards Mongolia and Inner Manchuria, but we have nothing to do with it. We are going to board the train to Siberia, which leaves at nine in the morning. We are finally going to enter Siberia.

Irkutsk

I was rather excited about visiting Siberia; it is not something one does every day. I kept looking at my watch often, waiting for six o'clock in the evening when we were scheduled to reach Irkutsk, the capital of Siberia. Finally at 6.35, I could spot Irkutsk station as we edged towards it. Wow! But there was nothing I could see except a small structure in a dilapidated condition. But what is this? I could hear voices floating in from all directions though I could not see anyone. I went towards the little building, trying to figure out what it was. Imagine my surprise when I entered it. This was the portal to enter the station that had been built underground. As one descended the fifty-odd steps, it was like entering a fish market. People were running hither-thither with their bundles and bags. What looked like a small place from the outside turned out to be quite an impressive railway station once you entered it. There were all kinds of facilities underground, including the ticket office, telegraph office, waiting rooms and a refreshment room. There was even a tunnel to cross over from one platform to another.

I was feeling hungry once again as I had not had anything except for cups of tea since we left Manchuria. 'It would be memorable to have a meal in the capital of Siberia,' I thought, and walked into the refreshment room. As soon as I sat down, a waiter approached me to take down my order. I pondered over the menu card but could not make any sense of it. Everything looked just the same. I told him to get me something to eat but he could not comprehend what I was saying. When I tried to mime it by bringing my hand close to my mouth, the waiter seemed to understand. He went and got me a box of cigarettes. It would have been funny if the joke was not on me. Finally, I had to make do with a cup of tea and a slice of cake.

Land of Ice and Snow

Now that we were in Siberia, do I even need to mention the cold? And if you are hungry, the cold does weird things to you. It seemed like a world gone mad on ice and snow! Wherever you looked, you could see mountains of snow. Not a speck of land which was not covered by snow. It was as if a white carpet had been laid out on the roads. The snow was two to three feet deep. If you tried to walk on it, you would sink to your knees. None of the trees had even a single leaf on them. On the other hand, snow was hanging from the branches, which made the trees seem like they were made of snow. Wherever you went, all you could see was snow, snow on roofs, snow on the roads, snow in houses, snow everywhere! All this was too tiresome for words. It was cold enough to freeze your bones. You would go so numb that it felt like your ears and nose had been chopped off.

I spent a most miserable night which I will never forget. Just imagine if one has to spend a whole winter here. Forget using a light blanket to cover oneself at night; instead, one would need a heavy rug, weighing a couple of tons. Even during the day, one cannot do without a heavy woollen overcoat lined on the inside with a thick layer of fur. A fur lining on the inside makes a big difference when compared to a coat without it. These overcoats are not a mere article of fashion to be flaunted. They could be the difference between life and death in this weather. Additionally, one has to wear headgear made from similar material, which covers practically the entire head and face. The outfit would not be complete without a pair of heavy boots that are also lined with fur on the inside. Having donned this attire, one can hardly walk or bend. But if one does not wear all this protective gear, one might end up dead and buried under those mountains of snow. During the months of December and January, the temperature drops to 40 degrees below zero. Where is one to get water to drink under these circumstances? But instead of water, one can get milk everywhere; and it is very cheap and extremely fresh. And our dear Siberians even wash their faces with milk during the harsh winters. If you wash your face with cold water, it might crack the skin. There is no question of taking a bath during winter. What is one to do if there is no water in the pipes? It just freezes up inside. In the morning, they wrap the pipe with straw and burn it. As the pipe heats up, small bits of ice first emerge from it before water starts flowing. Why bother with so much hassle?

Vehicles Without Wheels

How is one to go around in this cold weather? No motor cars or carriages with wheels are in sight during winter since such vehicles with wheels cannot move on snow. They have therefore fashioned sledges with iron springs, each of which can seat two people. A few sledges are designed to seat four people on seats that face each other. Instead of wheels, these vehicles have two iron runners that slide smoothly on the snow. They can be very easily hauled by horses. Since they do not have wheels, these sledges are rather low-slung like those little wooden carts on which children drag each other around in Navsari. But it is rather fun to ride these sledges. You just put your hand out and scoop up the snow. And one thing leads to another and we have a snowball fight! Strangely, during the summers, the snow and ice seem like a blessing. The summers are so harsh in Siberia that it becomes a different kind of hell. To escape the heat, the Siberians prefer to burrow themselves in ice houses that are specially constructed during the winters by digging underground chambers whose walls are lined with ice. Indeed, the world is full of strange things!

Fox Hunting in the Snow Mountains

The land of snow has got its own exclusive attractions. A roving sportsman could certainly have a good time. One of the more popular sports is the hunting of the Siberian fox. In our country, many hunters think no end of themselves after hiding up a tree and shooting down a passing tiger. They would be unable to shoot down a single fox. Fox hunting is a long-standing and well-known sport in the northern stretches of Siberia. The fur of the fox is much valued across Europe and fetches high prices. Its fur is considered to generate the most warmth and ladies across Europe feel rather chuffed when they wrap it around their necks.

The Siberian fox is hunted only during the winter season when its fur is most developed. At the same time, the heavy snow prevents the fox from running at top speed. It makes the job of the hunter much easier. After having surveyed the area in the morning and having determined that there are a lot of foxes around, the hunting team stakes the area and surrounds it with a thick rope from which red flags are hung at intervals. They fire a few rounds in the air to startle the foxes, which emerge from their hideouts and try to run away. But when they see the rope and the red flags, they get terrified. They keep running around in circles and stop only when they tire out. They are shot dead in that instant with a bullet aimed at either the forehead or the neck. If the bullet misses its mark, the fox runs away or tries to hide in the snow, making it difficult for the hunters to shoot it.

A Russian Wedding Procession

I must have been rather lucky on the day I entered Siberia, as I was able to witness a Russian wedding conducted in the traditional rustic fashion. Not everyone is as fortunate as me. In many ways, the customs followed in this Siberian wedding match our village customs. For instance, on the day of the wedding, the family of the groom goes in a procession to bring the bride to their village. The procession is led by girls, two in each row, followed by others who are three, four or five in a row. The procession wends its way through the village, and on reaching the village boundaries, it meets the bride's family who are led back into the village in the procession. The bride is slathered in red just like Hindu brides. She is then placed in a carriage around which a hemp rope is wound. The bride's parents hold a picture of her in their hands and lead the procession that now makes its way to the church. The people in the procession hold baskets, candles and flags in their hands, and dance as they proceed ahead. Not a man in the procession, be he married or single, walks alone. Every male has to be accompanied by at least one female, or else it is considered inauspicious for the couple who are going to be married. On reaching the church, a big dance takes place in the churchyard. The marriage party then enters the church, which is already packed with people. The wedding rituals take about an hour or so, and then the action shifts to the groom's residence where a big party is organized. Bottles upon bottles of Russian vodka are consumed. The newly married couple is toasted many times. After a while, the gifting session starts. As the bride's father stands holding a large sack in his hands, the guests drop a variety of gifts into it. It could be Chinese fur, shot glasses, or even a dead woodcock. The programme of toasting and gift-giving continues for three days to enable guests from distant villages to participate in the wedding festivities.

The Russian Mode of Worship

You would be surprised to learn that the priest who conducts the wedding is remunerated just like the dustoors in our villages who are offered eggs, bananas and pieces of meat for conducting minor rituals. A similar custom continues to prevail in Siberia. After the rituals are completed, people offer fruit, eggs or chicken as donations to the priest. On festival days, open-air services are held in Siberia. This service is generally conducted one month before Christmas when the sun makes a final appearance before the onset of winter. People gather in large numbers on this day. A senior priest comes with his retinue to the gathering. They stand facing the crowd and each of them holds an image of St Peter in their hands. The senior priest lights a candle before a large image of St Peter. Feeding an incense burner with wood shavings and agar, he prays before the image while the rest of the congregation echoes him. After the rituals are completed, the priests are offered the presents mentioned above.

The Russian Capital of Petrograd

There was no need to linger any longer in the bone-chilling cold of Siberia. I was to board the passenger train which left Irkutsk at seven in the morning. It felt like I was on the last stage of a rather tiresome journey. One fine evening, when I could spot the huge station of the Russian capital from a distance, I let out a huge sigh of relief. Amidst a shower of honks and whistles, our train, crossing many tracks, puffed into Petrograd station and came to a halt with a final shriek. The Russian porters were at it again! In the flash of an eye, the entire train was emptied out. However, this was not the end of the line for me. I was expecting to see a friend at the station but I could not spot him. As this was my first night in the Russian capital, I had no clue about the city. The station was enormous and the platforms extended for nearly a mile. Even if I tried to find him, I could wander around the whole day and we might still miss each other. I therefore decided to meet the station master in the hope that he might be able to help me. But how was I to find his office and tell him what I wanted in Russian? There were numerous offices in the station. If I asked someone for directions, he would look at me and flash a smile as if we knew each other from an earlier life, but no answer would be forthcoming. I just decided to walk into the first big office I saw. When I walked into the nearest office, the guard held me by the shoulder and tried to stop me from entering, as if saying: 'No admission without permission.'

It irritated me no end. If this had happened to me in my native village, I would have given it back to him and asked him to mind his manners. But what was I to do here? I just flashed my teeth at him and tried to explain my situation with a combination of words and gestures. This seemed to do the trick and I walked into the office. However, as soon as I entered the room, I realized it was not the station master's office. There were about a hundred girls in the room which resounded with a thousand clicks. Evidently, it was the telegraph office. Now that I had made an entry, what was the point in rushing out? All eyes were on me the moment I entered the room, wondering which planet I had landed from. I did not let it faze me and approached the closest lady, doffed my hat and asked for the station master. Did she understand a word of what I said? She just pointed me to another table and indicated I should go there. When I went to the next table, I got the same reply: a big nothing! I decided to try the opposite table. It seemed I was in luck as this lady uttered a few words of English. I immediately began to give her an account of my travels and was bombarded by questions from all the adjoining tables. After some discussion among themselves, they unanimously passed a resolution to escort me to the station master.

Escorted by my fair companion, I began walking towards the station master's office. It was a rather long walk. We passed by office after office and went up a couple of floors, but still did not reach his office. The station was quite a maze! Your legs would start to ache with all the walking we did. Finally, we reached the third floor and turned right to a room which was the station master's office. When I first saw him, the man with eyeglasses made such an impression on me that I began to wonder whether he was not the Russian czar himself. His bearing, his uniform, and his confident manners were quite a contrast to our poor station masters who futilely call out to their peons. It was a sight worth seeing. But he was very courteous towards me. Perhaps he thought I was a rajah from Hindustan. When I doffed my hat and wished him, he immediately offered me a chair. For about half an hour, we chatted on diverse subjects. There was a flurry of activity as he attempted to put a call through to the office of the British consul. I heaved a sigh of relief only when my friend came on the line and told me he would be at the station in an hour. I finally bid goodbye to the great station master with many bows and thank-yous and wended my way back downstairs with my fair companion. I still had an hour to kill at the station; I did not feel like saying goodbye to my fair companion and thought it best to wait at her office.

To my good luck, it was teatime at the office when we entered. The office was buzzing with arrangements for tea. I was wondering whether I would be offered some. All this walking around had parched my throat. Even as I was lost in my thoughts, a tinkling voice offered me a cup. Initially I made a show of reluctance, but soon gratefully accepted the offer. And then to my surprise, someone placed a piece of cake in front of me, another a sandwich, and yet another a delicious Russian sweet and biscuits. I was so hungry that I ate it all in a flash. Very soon, they gathered around my table and I felt as if I was surrounded by a bevy of Russian fairies. They asked me a lot of questions but I could not understand a word of what they said. However, what I did understand is that the Russians are second to none when it comes to hospitality.

The Attractions of the Russian Capital

Since Petrograd is the capital of Russia, you can well imagine the scale of its activities and the hustle-bustle here. However, I don't think the working hours would appeal to my taste. It is because of these strange working hours that my friend could not come to receive me at the station. During winter, the Russians get up at ten o'clock in the morning, have a cup of tea, and generally take it easy before having their breakfast at eleven or twelve. They then step out, perhaps to do some shopping, and finally reach their workplaces at one. Most offices open only at one or two in the afternoon, and similarly, most markets also open only after eleven in the morning. Aren't these people a happy lot? They leave for their offices at twelve or one with a packed lunch and are back home after eight in the evening, which is when most offices shut. Once they come home, they have high tea. Although it is a substantial meal, do not assume it is the final meal of the day. They normally have dinner at one or two in the night. This high tea is the equivalent of our afternoon tea. After tea, the Russians deck themselves up and step out. They might visit their friends or they could go to the theatre. The whole city seems to come alive at night. Most of the big shops are open late and the roads shine bright with electric lamps. The people also seem all agog with excitement. But do you know that there is yet another speciality about roaming here? One has to walk on one side of the road, either on the left or the right, depending on the direction in which you are walking. There is no question of colliding with anybody as you walk.

Because of these strange working hours, I was stranded in the station for a few hours. However, if one steps out of the station, walks about fifty paces, and turns right, one can find Hotel Grand where English is spoken. I could have gone there and saved myself a lot of hassle. Since this is the Russian capital, one need hardly mention its huge edifices and roads, which are lit up by electric light, or the beauty of its ladies whose rosy cheeks are further reddened by the cold. A village boy like me is bound to be attracted by this city. And if truth be told, I found it very difficult to leave the place!

But after a stay of eight days, I had to inevitably depart from the Russian capital with a heavy heart and a few teardrops in my eyes. Before leaving Petrograd, I had to go to the office of the British consul and get my passport stamped afresh. I headed towards the Finland station where I was to catch the express train that left at eight in the morning. There is also another express train from Petrograd to Sweden and Norway, which departs from the Finland station at nine in the night.

5

Scandinavia

We have digressed rather far from our journey. We might as well get back on track so that we can get to Sweden. Having left the Finland station by the eight o'clock train, I reached the Karunki station via Tornio at about eleven the next morning. Karunki is the last station on the Finnish side, from where one has to walk to Karungi which is in Sweden. They are about fifteen minutes from each other. Our passports were examined and stamped here. Having left Karungi, we reached Krylbo at about seven in the evening, where we had to alight to change trains. This was a real nuisance in the biting cold, especially since the next train was not departing from the railway station at Krylbo. We had to haul ourselves and our luggage on to a sledge carriage and get to Hallsberg station where another train was waiting for us. It is about thirty-six hours of travel from Karungi to Stockholm.

Nine Annas for a Cup of Tea and Twelve for Coffee

During the day, a plush saloon-cum-dining car had been attached to the train. How much do you think it cost to eat in this Swedish dining car? Even though I had heard from my grandmothers when I was young that Sweden was a very expensive place, I was not prepared for the prices here. A single meal in the dining car cost five rupees. If you felt like having a cup of tea at four in the afternoon, you would have to shell out nine annas. And coffee was twelve annas. Don't these people have any feelings of guilt? How could a person like me, who was used to paying one paisa for a cup of tea at the Irani restaurants of Mumbai, stomach these prices? If one had to stay in this area for a year, one would have to mortgage the whole of Navsari to raise funds for the trip. I have still not mentioned a rather novel experience I had during this train journey.

Experience at a Swedish Railway Restaurant

Every country is unique in its own way, but Sweden seems to take it to a different level. Out of the various difficulties I experienced during this long journey, I might as well mention one at this stage. Having left late at night, our train stopped at around eight in the morning at a station whose name I do not recall. My bones were frozen stiff in the morning cold and I was looking forward to having a steaming hot cup of tea. I had been pacing up and down the train carriage like a wild animal in its cage and kept an eagle eye out for any approaching station. And finally, the blessed station did arrive. I jumped off the train even before it came to a halt, shoved my hands into my trouser pockets, strode into the refreshment room, and sat down at a table. I expected that an eager waiter, in the hope of a large tip, would come running to take my order. Five minutes elapsed, and then ten! But there was no sign of any service. I restlessly wiped my face clean with a kerchief about fifty times and fidgeted in my seat. There was still no sign of anyone. My throat had dried up, and staring at the tea kettle which bubbled right in front of me made things worse. The

Russians in their heavy overcoats who were seated at the adjoining tables were sipping hot cups of tea. I almost felt like snatching the cups from their hands. Those who came after me were behaving as if they were in their own house. They would take cups and saucers from the table and fill them up with as much tea as they wanted, add milk and sugar according to their tastes, come back to their tables, and drink their tea with loud slurps. What kind of predicament was this? How long was I to sit here waiting for service? But no! Finally someone was willing to pay attention to me. The lady at the counter who was the cashier seemed to have noticed me. She came up to me and in a rather friendly tone asked me what I was doing there. I was taken aback. Here I had been waiting over fifteen minutes for a cup of tea and she wanted to know what I was doing there. Perhaps this was the Swedish fashion of treating guests. But she certainly did me a favour by talking to me and explaining the system. If I wanted to drink or eat anything, I just had to go and help myself. Initially, I thought she was making fun of me and was slightly annoyed. But no! This was how the place worked. It was later explained to me that one would have to serve oneself with anything one wanted to eat, make oneself a cup of tea or a dozen, and pay for what one had eaten or drunk. Where else was I to experience such freedom? I finally mustered up the courage to go to the table where plates of various sizes had been arranged and picked one up. I went to another table on which half a dozen yummy-looking dishes had been arranged and helped myself to a little from each of them. Then I went on to the adjoining table where I helped myself to a few slices from the mountain of bread that had been piled up. I picked up a knife and fork from the table opposite, and then moved on to a fourth table where cups and saucers had been placed. I carefully selected a large cup and made myself some tea, returned to my table and sat down to a sumptuous meal. Only after I had eaten did I come back to my senses. It was then that I asked about the system and found out that they did not have any waiters. Food and drink are arranged at various tables, and on other tables crockery and cutlery are laid out. The prices are mentioned in front of every dish–so much for a cup of tea and so much for a plate of food. You have to help yourself, keep track of what you have eaten, and pay for what you ate at the cash counter. What kind of honesty is this? If this system were to be implemented at the toddy shops of Navsari and in Mumbai's Irani restaurants, can you imagine the fun the scoundrels would have?

After enjoying a lot of new experiences, I reached the Swedish capital of Stockholm at about five in the evening. My plan was to spend a day in the capital. After having come to a distant country like Sweden, would it be proper to leave without taking a look at its capital? No! But first, I had to find a hotel for the night. Representatives of various hotels were present at the station. One would say that Hotel Grand is right in front of the king's palace, while another would shout out that Hotel Park is right opposite the station and just a minute's walk away. I was wondering whether one would have to adopt a lifestyle befitting a king at Hotel Grand and whether I would be able to afford to stay there. It cost four guineas per day for just the room without any board. It did not make any sense. I was a mere village boy and could hardly afford a regal lifestyle, and nobody would entertain someone like me there. I would stand out like a sore thumb. Perhaps Hotel Park opposite the station was better suited for me. It would cost just one guinea per day for the room and another guinea would suffice for food and drink for the entire day. After a lot of thought, I decided to stay at Hotel Park and shifted my luggage there.

Long-Necked Swedish Beauties

Only God knows why he elongated the faces of Swedish women! If there was a Swedish woman in a group of one hundred white ladies, she could be easily identified by her long and beautiful face. Having settled down in my room, I prettified myself just a little bit, applied cream to my hair, and after making sure it was not sticking up, I stepped out of the hotel. I wanted to make sure I looked decent. This was not Navsari where you could slink into any old toddy shop. I felt like strutting across the beautiful streets of Stockholm. After having walked down a few roads, I came across a building which looked like a palace and was lit brightly with electric lights. What could this place be? There was a lot of coming and going, and the sound of beautiful music being played by a band could be heard out on the street. I was rather tempted to go inside but I thought it prudent to first find out what the place was. When I asked a man who was standing nearby, he told me that it was a fashionable restaurant. I thought I might as well have dinner there. When was I going to get such an opportunity again?

I wiped my face clean, dusted my clothes and stepped in. Wow! Can you imagine the resplendence? As I had never been into such a posh restaurant before, I was dumbfounded. Everything was white in colour; the furniture was white, the tablecloths were white, and even the beautiful ladies who were sitting at the tables were coloured a pale white. White, white, and only white! An orchestra was playing melodious tunes on one side, while couples were dancing slowly on the other. Food and champagne were carefully arranged on tables. I was flustered. This did not seem to be a place for someone like me. I might sprain my leg while dancing. It was best to see such places from a distance.

Sweden to Norway

The next day, I saw a few of the famous sights in the Swedish capital, but I was not particularly impressed. There was no point in lingering in Stockholm as there was so much more to see and write about elsewhere. The following morning, I packed my stuff yet again and made my way to the station with my luggage. Travelling is not as easy as it seems to many people. But this is hardly the place to complain about my troubles. It is best to get on with my journey and see what fate has in store for me. I decided to catch the train to the Norwegian capital, Kristiania, which departed at thirty-six minutes past eight in the morning. Since it was only a twelve-hour journey from Stockholm to Kristiania, I reached Hotel Victoria at around eleven in the night. I spent the next day in the capital of Norway and caught the train to Bergen, which left Kristiania a little before midnight. Even before I was fully awake, the train chugged into the Bergen station around eleven the next morning. It felt like the beginning of the end of my journey; no more tiresome trains, no more whistles from the guard. All I had to do was bob in the ocean for a couple of days. Bergen is a beautiful town located on a little hill. A pleasant breeze was blowing in the morning and it was enough to refresh anybody. But was it in my fate to enjoy such breezes? I had very little time to get my passport in order. I needed to go to the British consulate to get my passport stamped afresh. Was that it? From there, I went straight to the steamer. I did not have to worry about my luggage as it had been sent directly from the station and loaded on to the steamer. I just had to twirl my swagger stick and take in the sights at the dock. Our dear little steamer *Australia* was ready to depart in a short while. When I reached the dock at about one in the afternoon, the steamship was already bobbing in the ocean waters. Though it might have been a small ship, it let out three or four sharp whistles as it departed, which shattered the peace of the little town. I was now back in the bosom of the ocean.

Typhoon in the North Sea

A departing steamer can be great fun, especially when there are beautiful girls with moist eyes waving goodbye with their kerchiefs to young men standing on the upper decks with their hands in their trousers and a cigarette dangling from their mouths. But let us move on. I was rather hungry now. I had forgotten to eat anything because of all the running around at Bergen and was looking forward to a hearty meal. Just then, the lunch bell rang and all the passengers rushed to the dining room. Unfortunately, this first meal on the ship also proved to be the last one. By the evening, our little ship was rolling heavily in the waters and seemed to have run into one of those storms for which the North Sea is famous. It was as if the steamship *Australia* was a mere bubble floating on the surface of the water–it could burst at any moment. The violence of the sea seemed to be getting worse with every passing minute.

Can you imagine the miserable condition of the passengers? They were queued outside the toilet to rinse the vomit out of their mouths. At night, it seemed the ship was flying in the air one moment and was diving deep into the water the next. The speed of the wind increased gradually. The dark night painted a terrible scene as black waves dashed against the steamer with a loud noise. Almost everybody on board seemed to be enveloped by a feeling of terror. As there was always the danger of an attack by submarines at night, no lights were permitted on the steamer, which seemed to make the situation worse. The passengers were in a terrible state. The condition of the poor ladies was very pitiable. The sight of them throwing up every other minute was rather depressing. Everybody on board wondered if we would be able to survive until the next morning. But as they say, nature defies prediction! The terrible, terrifying night also passed, and we finally limped into the beautiful harbour of New Castle after a miserable journey of forty hours. The passengers heaved a sigh of relief and congratulated each other on their good fortune. It was as if they had been handed a fresh lease of life. The ladies, who had suffered the most from seasickness, were particularly grateful to have survived the storm. The beaming faces all around reflected the joy of having emerged unscathed from this perilous experience.

6

Arrival in England

My heart was beating rapidly with excitement. After having boarded the train to London at two in the afternoon, I was in a strange state of expectation.

My First Steps in England

Was it an ordinary matter to finally reach London, the original vilayat for us Indians? I had grown up hearing so much about the place and its personalities that London seemed to be something out of this world. I was rather impatient to see the city. Who among us would not like to go to vilayat? The very mention of it leaves many of us salivating with expectation. When a man returns home after a trip to vilayat, he seems to be in seventh heaven and his mother struts around town with her nose in the air. Is it therefore strange that a simpleton like me was so excited? I would get to join the smart set in London and hear the king's band play at Hyde Park. My heart leapt with joy in expectation of this blissful state of affairs. I harassed the guard by repeatedly asking him when we would reach London. For the umpteenth time, I washed my face so I would look fresh when I arrived in London. They should not form a wrong impression about me based on first sight. This was my first time on the trains of vilayat, and I was enjoying myself by bouncing on the velvet seats. I visited the lavatory a few times to take in the fragrance of the soap placed there. I dirtied half a dozen crisply ironed kerchiefs by wiping down my hands and legs. What a difference between the ramshackle carriages of the Indian railways and these trains, where even the third class is good enough for a king. When would I experience such a day in Hindustan? Ah! When will you, my dear proud Hindustan, attain these levels? But let's leave such depressing thoughts aside for now.

London in Darkness

Our train entered the world-famous city of London at around eight at night when it was enveloped in complete darkness. When the train halted at the station, there was a flurry of activity from the porters and the representatives of the prominent hotels of London. Since it was already rather late, I decided to stay in Hotel Metropole for the night. I thought I might as well walk to the hotel with my companion and take a first look at the fabled city of London. But the minute I stepped out of the station, it was all disappointment! For a minute I thought the Siberian cold might have spoilt my eyesight. London seemed all dark and droopy. All my excitement and expectations evaporated into nothing. It was so pitch dark that the broad streets of London seemed frightening and scary. Why was such a large city enveloped in darkness? It seemed that the bright electric lights of the London municipality were less powerful than the dim lights of my dear Navsari. As the glass shades of the street lamps had been painted black, they cast a rather weak light on the roads. The windows of all the shops and houses were covered with black curtains to prevent any light from escaping on to the streets. It was as if a dark curtain had been drawn over this once colourful city. People were afraid to venture out in this scary darkness. But what was the reason for this darkness? It was the war, this all-destructive war! Gay London was being threatened by aerial monsters–German Zeppelins–which were all too eager to destroy the city. The residents already wore a scared look after having been terrorized by the Zeppelin raids a few times. If a child threw a tantrum, the mere mention of the word 'Zeppelin' would quieten it down. It was as if troubles were being showered over the beautiful city of London.

We walked through the dark streets and finally reached Hotel Metropole a little after nine o'clock. It was considered to be one of the more fashionable hotels of London. The sight of its six-storey building with its six hundred magnificent rooms would leave any country bumpkin goggle-eyed. There are other hotels in London that are grander than the Metropole, such as Hotel Cecil with its thousand bedrooms and a dining room big enough to seat 1,500 to 2,000 people at one go. Only the poorest–either a Lord so-and-so or a Baronet such-and-such–seem to go there! If you told anyone you were staying at Hotel Cecil, your prestige would shoot up ten times, such is its fame. How much do you think these hotels earn? It is said that such hotels clock a profit of one to two million rupees per year. No big deal! All the waiters seem to be dirt poor! Ha! If word got around in Navsari about the salaries these waiters received, they would think I had gone mad; utterly, completely mad! I am rather scared to mention the numbers. They can earn as much as five hundred to one thousand rupees just in tips besides their regular salaries. But the situation had turned upside down during the war. This famed hotel wore a very different look. It had been turned into a military office for the various war departments, including the YMCA (Young Men's Christian Association). And the waiters whose income used to be as large as that of our governors have also disappeared. Instead of cleaning utensils in the kitchen, they were cleaning their guns on the battlefield.

THE WESTERN FRONT

7

I Become a Tommy

Fate can have fantastic things in store for you. Who could have imagined that I was destined to be a soldier and that I would fight numerous battles under the most trying circumstances? It was in the realms of fantasy. When I think back on the soldierly life I led, it still fires me up. To be sure, I had been inspired during my childhood days by the tales of heroes in the *Shahnama* and the *Burjornama*. The descriptions of exploits of valour and courage in these books were permanently etched in my mind and inspired me to fight many a battle. This enthusiasm led me to the famous Head Recruiting Office in Whitehall to volunteer for the British Army, and this opened a new page in my life. I should confess I was refused admission in the first instance. They suggested I contact the India Office and join the Indian Army. Well, I was not one to be fazed by this rejection. To cut a long story short, after a million struggles, I was finally recruited into the British infantry as a 'private' in the 24th Middlesex Regiment, which was then based in Northampton. Even before I joined the regiment, I was granted four days of leave. On its expiry, I headed towards Euston station to board the train for Northampton where I would take up my new assignment.

At seven o'clock in the evening, we reached Northampton station and were asked to proceed to the battalion headquarters which was then based in the famous Franklin's Gardens. On reporting my arrival, I was admitted into the D Company, and like every newly enlisted soldier, I was assigned a number. Mine was 3213.

Before proceeding ahead, we might as well understand how the armed forces are organized. Let us first consider a battalion, which may include 1,000 to 1,200 men; it is usually divided into six companies. The first is the Headquarter Company, the second is the A Company, the third is the B Company, the fourth is the C Company, the fifth is the D Company, and so on. In some cases, this might go on till the H Company. Each company is headed by a company commander who is assisted by four officers, known as toon (platoon) commanders. A company is further divided into four platoons, each headed by a toon commander who has a toon sergeant assigned to help him. Further, a platoon is made up of four sections, each headed by a non-commissioned officer who is responsible for that section. Besides the company commander, each company is also assigned a company sergeant major and a company quartermaster sergeant. The quartermaster sergeant is responsible for provisions, arms and ammunition, the payment of salaries, and the uninterrupted supply of all manner of materials.

In like fashion, besides the commanding officer, each battalion is assigned a second commanding officer, an adjutant, a lieutenant quartermaster, a regimental sergeant major and a regimental quartermaster sergeant. These officers are the heads of the various departments of the battalion. A 'fighting battalion' is organized in this manner, and four of these battalions together form a 'brigade', which is commanded by a brigadier general. Each brigade is also assigned an artillery unit. Three to four brigades combine to form a 'division' headed by a major general. Finally, divisions are part of a corps, also known as the 'army corps'. This is headed by the corps commander, a very senior military officer of the grade of lieutenant general. The army corps consists of fighting units from the infantry, cavalry and artillery. All these units–battalions, brigades, divisions and corps–are numbered and are always referred to by these numbers. Many of us seem to think that a battalion is the same as a regiment, but this is a mistake; in fact, many battalions make up one regiment. For example, the Middlesex Regiment consists of thirty-six battalions and each of them is identified by the name 'Middlesex' and a number.

The Military Camp

Although this might take us away from our main narrative, let us take a look at how the military camp is organized, so that we understand how the army actually operates. This was the start of my military life, and I was making this kind of sortie for the first time in my life. Everything was new, unfamiliar and astonishing; the shock almost paralysed me for a while. I was still in deep sleep, ensconced in my warm blanket, when the accursed bugle went off; this was the reveille, sounding the morning wake-up call. It was loud enough to puncture my eardrums. Some of the men were already up and about, spitting on their boots to work up a polish; others were still yawning, stretching, swearing and shouting. Soon enough, boots were flying all over the place. Those five-pounders could break your jaw if they landed square on your face. 'Better safe than sorry,' I thought, and got up and sat silently huddled in a corner.

This was my first experience of this kind of life, and I must confess that I did not particularly warm up to it. I did not know a soul in the room; not a friend or an acquaintance with whom

I could amuse myself. Well, I had no option but to grit my teeth and take it as it came. I thought I would sit silently and survey the action, but there were many things which had to be done that could not wait. The blanket had to be folded in just that manner. One of the guys had to pick up the broom and clean up the place; then on to the washing area to clean the body. But by then the bugle screamed once again. What now? The parade. This was just the first parade of the morning, called the 'roll call parade'. One had to assemble in the designated place, and once the orderly sergeant issued the orders for 'Fall in', everybody had to stand in line. When your name was called out, you had to answer back. Then for the next half an hour, a routine of physical exercises was conducted to stamp out the cold. The orders for 'Dismiss' would be barely issued when all the boys would break into a desperate run, like a pack of wild animals. By the time we reached our quarters, the bugle would sound out yet again: Breakfast! This was the one bugle which was always welcomed by the Tommies. Armed with our forks and knives, we had to assemble yet again on the parade ground from where we were escorted by the non-commissioned officer to the dining room. This was my first experience of army food and I did not like a thing about it. Once we were seated at the dining table, slices of bread and bacon were served with cups of tea. Try as I might, I could not get the food down my throat. My mouth felt rotten. But what was to be done? By this time, the orderly officer was on his rounds, accompanied by the orderly sergeant. They would come to each table, look us in the eye, and ask us, 'Any complaints?', to which one of the guys would immediately get up and reply, 'No complaints, sir!', and they would move on to the next table. Having finished breakfast, one had to get going right away because it was immediately followed by the second parade of the day.

We had about half an hour to clean our jackets and polish our buttons to a shine; using a combination of spit and polish, the boots had to be worked up to a mirror finish; the bayonet on the rifle had to be burnished fifty times to sharpen it. Just as these tasks were about to be completed, the bugle would sound yet again and we would have to head towards the parade grounds.

On the first day, however, one did not have to report for the second parade; all new arrivals had to go to the quartermaster store to be issued uniforms and other related military paraphernalia. When I heard this order, I heaved a huge sigh of relief because all this hustle-bustle and running around did not appeal to my disoriented mind. Oh, if only God gave me a pair of wings with which I could fly to Navsari and burrow into a safe corner! But hell, was my Lady Luck so kind? Well, at nine o'clock in the morning, I set off once again for the clothing parade. I was under the impression that all I had to do was report there, pick up what was issued right away, and then I would get some time for myself. But it was not to be! When I arrived at the quartermaster store, there was already a long queue of Tommies who were waiting at the door. I was wondering how long it would be before my turn. And it turned out to be worse than I had feared. I had joined the queue at nine, and then the clock struck twelve noon and then one, but the situation still seemed bleak. We had no option but to keep waiting outside in the sun. Nobody would listen to our complaints, much less redress them. A freshly minted Tommy ahead of us swore at the quartermaster only to be immediately hauled off by two men to the guardroom, actually the military prison. This was enough to throw cold water on any plans of remonstrance we might have had. Thankfully, the bugle for lunch sounded just then. We were indeed glad to get this break, but we were asked to reassemble at two o'clock at the same place. When the sergeant gave an almighty roar—Dismiss!—we dispersed.

At about half past three, we emerged from St James's Park, each of us hauling a big kitbag filled with khaki clothes over one shoulder, while the other hand was weighed down by standard-issue trench boots that felt like a hundred pounds. We, however, got a very warm reception from the general public as we walked back to our camp singing our new anthem, 'Old Kitbag and Smile'. The local residents would come running out of their houses to greet us and repeatedly offer their congratulations on our new uniforms, which would fire us up and we would march more energetically. It was now time for us to say goodbye to our old clothes and fully enter into our new avatars. We bid a final farewell to our ties and collars. The skintight varnished boots disappeared from sight, and in their stead we had to struggle into those twenty-pound military boots studded with nails. In the space of half an hour, the last vestiges of our previous lives had been brushed off completely and we were well and truly on our way to beginning a new chapter of our lives. Twirling an army-issue truncheon, and saluting every officer we met on the way, we stamped our heavy boots on our way to Kingsley Park to spend the first evening of our new lives.

Battalion Order

It is best if we obtain some understanding of military training before we head towards the battlefields. A battalion order is an order from the commanding officer and is issued every evening. When the bugle sounds the issue of the battalion order, the orderly sergeant of each company has to make a dash to the orderly room. The regimental sergeant major dictates the orders to each of them—the morning wake-up times, the parade timings for the company, the schedule of the company officers, the rota for the quarter guard, the number of men required, etc. Details of men sick in the hospitals are also given; besides, new recruits are allotted to each company. The orderly sergeant for the next day is also designated in this evening order, and if there are to be any inspections by the commanding officer, they are also notified in the battalion order. However, the detailed orders for the parades of the company are issued by the company commander after roll call at night.

If it is a Sunday, then you are sort of okay, or else just the thought of waking up in the morning is enough to get you down. At half past five in the morning, the bugle sounds reveille loud enough to make you sit upright on your bed. If not the bugle, then it is the regimental band which marches through the entire camp twice or thrice a week, creating a right royal racket. To be sure, when one first hears the notes from those instruments, one is lulled further into the deeper realms of sleep; but as the music gets louder, one has no option but to get up. And indeed, one is better off getting up right away rather than facing the music later on. A late entry into the parade grounds would earn one a thorough dressing down from the non-commissioned officer besides a charge of 'late on parade' for which the commanding officer would hand out 'extra drill' as punishment. A newbie like me could hardly afford such a situation. The first parade was followed by breakfast, and immediately thereafter, the bugle would sound the second parade. Sometimes the orders for the second parade would, instead of an ordinary drill, involve a 'full marching order', when we had to be fully togged out. If the parade was scheduled for half past nine in the morning, one had to be present on the grounds by nine o'clock. After the usual calling out of names, the sergeant major would do his rounds, checking our attire: are the buttons on our tunics shining or not; are our gun slings properly cleaned; are all our caps in exactly the same position; whether the 'packs' on our backs are perfectly aligned; and to top it all, he would check if we had shaved ourselves clean and smooth in the morning. If he had the slightest of doubts, he would not hesitate to run his hands along our cheeks. Once the sergeant major was done with his inspection, the company commander or the toon commander would repeat it all over again. This would be followed by the most minute inspection of the rifle to see if it was in perfect working condition. If there was the slightest stain or speck of dirt in the barrel or on the magazine, you were sure to be severely punished. The attire of every soldier, from his cap to his socks, had to be perfectly uniform. There was absolutely no freedom to express your style. You had no choice but to follow the orders verbatim. After all these inspections had been carried out to everybody's satisfaction, we had to march 'slope arms' to the parade ground, which was about a mile away from camp, where the morning drill would actually begin. We were divided into smaller groups: one group would practise 'bayonet fighting', another would do physical drills for an hour, a third would train in rifle exercises, while a fourth would go through the 'squad drill' which involved marching endlessly to the tune of 'left, right, left, right'. These drills, which went on till twelve noon, would drain every last ounce of energy from us. At twelve, we would again get into formation and march back to camp. By the time we reached camp, the bugle would sound the lunch hour. After lunch, one had just about enough time to clean the knife and fork before one had to tog out yet again, because at quarter to two, the bugle would invite us to the parade grounds. We marched out yet again to the parade grounds with our rifles on our shoulders. After the morning inspection routine was repeated, we were drilled for two hours in 'repeat loading' and 'standing load', besides the extremely exacting company drill exercises. At four in the evening, we would head back and have a cup of tea;

then we were done for the day! Occasionally, we would be taken for night operations or for a night march. If not, we could go wherever we wanted for the evening but had to be back in camp by nine o'clock at night. At half past nine, the bugle would sound the 'roll call parade' when the orderly would shriek out–'Fall in!'–and our names would be called out yet again to check if each of us was back in camp. After this roll call, one could not leave camp. At quarter to ten, the bugle sounded 'lights off', when all manner of lights had to be extinguished and one had to get into bed. After this point, if anybody lit any light or attempted to walk about, he would be arrested by the military police.

The Commanding Officer's Saturday Inspection

In military circles, the very mention of the accursed word 'inspection' is enough to drive you bonkers. You have an inspection for everything: an inspection when you sneeze, an inspection when you eat, an inspection when you wash your hands, inspection this, inspection that, and even inspections of inspections. Where is it to end? Every morning, the orderly officer goes on his rounds of the entire encampment. His first stop is the cookhouse to check if the utensils used for cooking have been properly cleaned, if the food has been properly cooked, and if the rations have been correctly distributed among the various companies. He then turns towards the sleeping quarters to check if all the mattresses have been properly folded up and arranged. During every meal, he visits each table to check the food which is served, and on the pretext of checking, he does not miss out on pouring himself a glass of my beloved beer from the canteen! Everything is inspected all the time, but the running around which happens during the Saturday inspection has to be seen to be believed. The Saturday inspection by the chief commanding officer is scheduled to start at ten o'clock in the morning, but orders to 'stand-to' are issued at nine. At ten, the bugles sound the commencement of the inspection by the commanding officer. In his wake, there is a huge tail that runs after him. An adjutant hangs on to every word he utters, and notes down every strength and weakness in his notebook. There is also a medical officer who is quite willing to sniff at even onions and potatoes. The orderly officer is also present in his retinue, but the sergeant major has to bear the brunt of this inspection, while the quartermaster runs around like mad to ensure things are what they should be. The orderly sergeant, in his full uniform, is running ahead of the commanding officer, preceded by the bugler who keeps a very fast pace. Bringing up the rear is a group of a dozen orderly non-commissioned officers. The entire camp is a sight to see on this day; if, by any chance, things are not as per the rules, it might as well be your funeral. Everybody is on tenterhooks, just waiting for the inspection to be completed. All soldiers are expected to be in full uniform and standing by their mattresses, all neatly folded up as per regulation. If there is the slightest deviation from the norm, the sergeant major immediately jots down the poor soldier's name. He is later hauled up in front of the company commander, and he can be sure of being handed out a stiff punishment. As the inspection draws to a close, one can see the buglers running around like crazy all over camp. When they triumphantly sound the completion of the inspection, their racket echoes across the entire camp and is enough to make you deaf; however, just hearing it gives everybody a fresh lease of life. After this inspection, there is still the morning 'kit' inspection to be faced. The mattress is rolled out, the hold-all opened up, and each one arranges his 'kit' (army uniform), all neatly folded up as per regulation, ready for inspection. Every little item is to be displayed–a jacket and trousers, two shirts, one towel, a pair of boots, a cardigan, the mess tin, cleaning brushes, razor–but not according to one's whim and fancy. The jacket is to be folded up and placed in such a manner that its brass buttons are visible. Every item is to be placed at just the right place. The equipment is to be cleaned and loaded with blanks; the brass buckles of the gun strap are to be polished; the gun is to be hung at the head of the bed. Needless to add, the bayonet is to be fixed to the end of the rifle. If any item is missing, a note is immediately made of it and its cost is deducted from our salary.

Besides the usual parades, the army has yet another parade to disburse wages. This is the one parade which is welcomed by the soldiers. The 'pay parade' is held only once a week, on Fridays. However, the drink-happy soldiers look forward to it from Monday itself. First, you are flush with money on that day, and second, you can give a miss to the usual 'left, right, left, right' parade. Once the money comes into your hands, you can leave camp. Privates assemble at two o'clock in the afternoon in front of the office of the quartermaster; everybody stands in line following the alphabetical order of their names. When your name is called, you enter the office, salute the officer, stuff the money into your pocket, sign against your name, offer yet another salute, and then scoot.

8

To the Western Front

We seem to have lost our way and digressed very far from our main narrative to which we must get back. After six months of intensive training at Northampton, our regiment was ordered to move to the famous military station of Aldershot. I was a member of the 'advance party'. Each member of the advance party was carrying only his personal luggage. Before the arrival of the regiment, we had to set up tents and clean the camp. When any regiment moves from one place to another, it is divided into three parties: the advance party which proceeds to the destination first and ensures that everything is in order, the 'main body' which consists of most of the regiment, leaving behind a 'rearguard' which cleans up the encampment and leaves it in a state of order before joining the regiment.

The Famous Military Command of Aldershot

There must hardly be a soldier alive who has a soft corner for Aldershot. The commander of this place was considered to be an extremely strict officer. But at any rate, we were not to stay there for very long. We had already undergone the prescribed military training. Dark clouds were gathering around us and on one accursed morning, we were among the five hundred selected for the draft proceeding to the battlefields of France. Before departing from Aldershot, we were treated to a sumptuous dinner at the expense of our regiment. This was our last meal in England, and for this very reason, it was a most exquisite and elaborate spread. We drank an enormous number of toasts, since nobody was sure who among the five hundred of us would return alive, in one piece. After the meal, the bugle sounded the assembly on the parade ground. The brass band belonging to our regiment was ready and waiting for us outside. Do I need to say anything about the crowd that had gathered? Once everybody had assembled on the parade ground, the commanding officer gave an inspirational speech, offered his good wishes and sent us on our way. To the sound of cheers and the strains of music from the band, we marched towards the station.

Departure from Aldershot

As our draft was to proceed to the killing fields of France, both sides of the road were lined with crowds who had come to see us off. Women leaned out of windows and greeted us with shouts of 'Hurray!' Buffeted by all these sounds, we finally reached the station that was overflowing with people. There was still over an hour to kill before our train was to depart. Our brass band played sweet tunes to amuse the public. At the station, girls would offer us baskets full of chocolates and cigarettes. For free! Would you believe it? In short, we were a very pampered lot and the object of well-deserved sympathy. When the train halted at the platform, we immediately boarded the compartment reserved for us. As we hardly had any luggage with us, we did not have to trouble the porters! We carried the rifle, bayonet and the associated equipment in our hands. The pack on our backs contained an overcoat, a metal dinner plate, a mess tin, an undershirt, a pair of underpants, and two pairs of socks. This paraphernalia made up all of our capital. Amidst the shouts of 'Hurray!' and the ear-splitting noise of whistles, our train chugged out of the station and we bid a final adieu to the allurements and attractions of England.

A Warm Welcome in France

After leaving Aldershot, we reached the Folkestone station at about three o'clock at night and made our way to the rest house on foot. As we had to leave the train here and board a steamer for France, we broke our journey for one night. We had tea and supper and waited for daybreak. Not having the luxury of a bed or a mattress, we just lay down in our clothes and spent a few restless hours. At five in the morning, the bugle sounded the wake-up call. We roused ourselves immediately, washed and shaved, polished our shoes and buttons, and cleaned our rifles. It took us almost an hour to get into shape before we proceeded ahead after having breakfast. This station sees a traffic of thousands of soldiers coming and going every day, but still everything happens like clockwork. The cook room is staffed with ladies who have stepped out of their homes and rolled up their sleeves to serve the nation in desperate times. The grandest hotels of Folkestone have been requisitioned by the military; we had a nice view of the sea from the windows which gladdened our hearts after the miserable night. Behind us were the cliffs of Folkestone; the little houses on them made a pretty picture. We began making preparations to embark on the steamer. All put together, we were about two thousand soldiers who were to make the journey. We started walking to the docks in batches.

At the pier, two steamers were waiting for us, puffing smoke from their bellies. We embarked on an 8,000-ton steamer.

Not having been provided with anything by way of seating arrangements, we just plonked ourselves on the deck, in the manner of goats, wherever we could find a little space. We set sail for France at forty-five minutes past nine, accompanied by cheers from the ships nearby and a colourful shower of handkerchiefs. In this final hour of our departure, not a single one of us was dejected or depressed. In fact, many were lustily singing for most of the journey; others were playing cards. After a voyage which lasted five hours, we reached the French port of Boulogne around three in the afternoon. On alighting, we said our final goodbyes to the coast of France and marched through the roads of this famous city towards our camp. As we marched down the streets of Boulogne-sur-Mer, we received the most enthusiastic reception from its residents. From windows and open doors, balconies and balustrades, and in all the streets and localities, the residents of this city welcomed us warmly to their country. It was as if the hearts of the French people had been pledged to British soldiers. Many of them waved the Union Jack while others waved kerchiefs. Some of the more forward French girls and boys marched hand in hand with the Tommies. After a very enjoyable experience in this French city, we reached our camp, which was lined with row upon row of tents. Each tent was to house ten soldiers. We were only supplied raw provisions in this camp, and we had to cook them ourselves. Some of us went to chop up firewood, while others went to collect water to make tea. After a day of rest, we were ordered to quit the camp. We again packed our stuff, hoisted our packs on to our backs, and were ready to march. I think the material we had to carry during a full marching order, including our weapons, must have weighed at least eighty pounds. Hauling this weight, we trudged up to the station at Boulogne. We were to travel by train to the major military encampment at Ertaup. There was a train already waiting for us on the platform. Excellent arrangements had been made at the station canteen for our breakfast and we tucked into a hearty meal. After a none-too-pleasant journey, we finally reached the station at Ertaup at five o'clock in the evening. A gargantuan encampment with thousands of tents extending in every direction had been erected there and a hundred thousand soldiers were camped there. Army personnel were assigned to the battlefields from this camp as and when required. Before soldiers were actually sent to fight, they were given additional training here. There was no shortage of anything in this camp. The food provided to the rank and file here was better than that in England. Though the soldiers actually fighting on the front regularly faced acute shortages, immense quantities of food were regularly and unthinkingly dumped into garbage bins here. On the other hand, there was an acute shortage of living quarters in this camp. Each tent housed twenty-one soldiers along with their fighting equipment. There was hardly any space to lie down to sleep at night. You could not move an inch or turn over in your sleep without waking the person sleeping next to you. To help pass the time in such trying circumstances, the YMCA would organize a variety of entertainment shows. Concerts were held every day, with performers specially invited from London. In this manner, the hardships of the day were sought to be diminished by these colourful extravaganzas.

Towards the Battlefields

After spending eight days in this camp, we proceeded to the actual fighting area to join our regiment. Our regiment was already involved in the fighting and we were sent to reinforce the existing troops. When we reached the station at Ertaup, we saw cattle trucks (goods compartments) waiting to receive us instead of the usual train. All our journeys henceforth would be in these cattle trucks. Each compartment was packed with forty soldiers in the manner of goats. Not even a bench, no nothing! We just dumped our luggage on the floor and sat on it. Some of the boys poked their heads out of the netting just like a herd of sheep or goats. In spite of the pitiable situation we found ourselves in, there was an element of novelty to it and it was clear that we were about to turn a new page in our lives. Our 'Punjab Mail' chugged on at full speed, but the compartments were such that we fell over each other and had a terrible time of it. All we could do was think of God! We spent a most miserable night on the train, and at about three in the morning, we reached Maricourt station. We had to stop here for a little while before proceeding further, but as per military rules, our train could not halt at the station. We finally stopped about half a mile ahead, where we halted until daybreak. All of us just sprawled on the ground, using the railway tracks as our pillows, and spent a most awful night. This was the first of our many bitter experiences. At sunrise, there was a flurry of activities; we obtained hot water from the engine to make tea. Soon, we received orders to proceed ahead to our destination, Donercourt.

Devastation in France

En route, we were ordered to halt at a village where we could have breakfast. It was a small village with no large buildings that could house us; we just gathered in front of a dilapidated house. Its frontage had about a thousand holes in it. But under the circumstances, it was rather strange that it was still standing. We lit our fires to fry bacon and make tea. Not being sure when our next meal would be, we ate to our heart's fill. We then hoisted our luggage and began the long march to Donercourt. This was our first long march and we experienced a great many difficulties on the way. Quite a few of the poor soldiers would stumble and fall, but there was nobody to care about them. It was each man to himself and there were many stragglers who could not keep up. This long march was the most exhausting as we had to haul our entire kit ourselves. At five in the evening, after suffering many a hardship, we finally managed to reach Donercourt, where our regiment was based. When we entered this village, we were greeted by the strangest sights: most of the structures had been reduced to rubble by cannonballs; the roofs of many of the houses had collapsed, while some of them were left hanging precariously. We were to lodge in one of these houses. Before we could unload our luggage, the new arrivals were assigned to different companies. This was to be our first night in this devastated village, which was about ten miles away from the actual scene of battle. All through the night, the sound of artillery and gunfire reverberated in the skies above us. Besides, huge rats which had been displaced from their usual haunts by the war harassed us in our sleep. After joining our newly assigned companies, we had to fall in with the prescribed routine of activities. The first of these was the morning inspection of new arrivals by the commanding officer. Although the inspection was scheduled for ten o'clock in the morning, preparations were afoot from six. The company officer would issue orders to the sergeant major—'Company on parade at half past nine'. In turn, the sergeant major would order the toon sergeant to be ready at nine o'clock. This was a 'full marching order'—we had to be fully togged with our entire kit and wait on the parade ground for a whole hour before the inspection commenced. Immediately after the inspection by the commanding officer, we were to be examined by the regimental doctor; this meant waiting in line for yet another hour. If one was lucky, one's turn would be before lunch, or else one would have to join the queue again at two in the afternoon. After the medical examination, we would have to rush for lunch. At the war front, our daily rations were as follows: a slice of bacon, fried or boiled as the case may be, and a cup of tea for breakfast. It would have been stupid to expect any variety in this fare; in fact, on some days, even this would not be forthcoming. Dinner was at one in the afternoon, which consisted of our 'favourite' bully beef, boiled stew and potatoes. Tea was at five in the evening when a tin of jelly was to be shared by eleven men. On most days, instead of bread, we were provided with very hard biscuits. Bread would sometimes not be available for days on end. After the morning meal, each soldier would have to wash his utensils clean and dry them, and wait for the orderly officer to inspect them. This waiting business could take up half an hour or so. After this inspection, we were supposed to fill one of these utensils with water, which was available at a distance of about half a mile. Most of our time was taken up by activities of this sort. Just as we completed these menial tasks, orders would be barked out: 'On parade!' For God's sake! Heaping a thousand curses on the damned war, we would trudge out to the parade grounds with our rifles on our shoulders. Since we had joined new platoons, we would have to learn a new set of drills. After five in the evening, we could take a walk in the woods or set about washing our clothes. Not a sight of Mumbai's Apollo Bunder or Chowpatty, or London's Hyde Park where we could stroll casually in the evening. From the time we woke up to the time we went to sleep, we had to keep our rifles in sight, always at hand or on our shoulders. It was even our sleeping partner.

9

The Killing Fields of France

It was not in our fate to enjoy even these mean favours for long, as our battalion was soon asked to move closer to the battlefront. At about 1.30 in the afternoon, we made our way towards Fricourt with our kits. With thousands of soldiers and vehicles going to and fro, the traffic on this road was to be seen to be believed. We reached Fricourt at about five in the evening after a forced march.

First Experience on the Battlefields

We spent the night in the open. We were practically on the battlefields—no possibility of tents or buildings to stay in! All you had to do was find a flat piece of ground and lie down; no need to bother with bedding and blankets! You had to pull a waterproof blanket over yourself and go off to sleep. The iron helmet served as a pillow and your overcoat was the comforter. There was no need to undress or remove your boots; you slept as you were. But did we have any hope of sleeping? It got colder as the night advanced and the rain made matters worse. The cold would numb your legs beyond imagination and the pitter-patter of the rain would irritate you through the night. Nowhere to shelter, our only option was to get wet all through the night. And by the time we woke up, our bodies were fully stiff. To top it all, the firing of guns through the night would puncture our eardrums. The din they created frightened us to the core of our hearts. The sky would be so bright that it seemed like it was on fire. I cannot bring myself to describe the fear and terror with which we spent our first night on the battlefield as we sat up looking far into the horizon. There was not a moment of respite from the artillery fire. How could soldiers like us, who were experiencing all of this for the first time, even hope to sleep? When we finally woke up shivering at dawn, we had no water to wash ourselves. On the battlefront, each soldier was provided with one bottle of water every day, and there were orders for it to be used only for drinking. If anybody had water left over in their bottles from the previous day, they could use it for washing up. At some distance, there was a small pond covered with algae; as we had no other vessels, we would fill up our iron helmets with water from the pond and use it to wash our faces. On other days, we would use the dew collected on our overcoats through the night to dab on our faces.

The Explosive Power of Cannons

After a few days at this place, we were asked to advance further. From now on, all movement was to be done only at night. Our destination was Match Wood, the reserve trenches about five miles up ahead. Just when we set off, it started to rain. We were finding it extremely difficult to make our way through the mud and slime in the dark of the night. There were huge depressions along our route, which had been created by artillery firing. This area had earlier been in the possession of the Germans, and the evidence of intensive hand-to-hand combat could be seen strewn all over. It was quite obvious that these hundreds of cavities and depressions had been created by 15-inch artillery guns. Before we go further ahead, let us consider these highly destructive weapons that were used in the war. These 15-inch guns became very famous as instruments of mass destruction in this bloodthirsty war. When one of the shells shot from these guns hit the ground, it would create a depression about six feet deep and six feet across. These 15- and 18-inchers could make a mountain shudder. Their barrels were large enough to accommodate a man. From the rearguard, they could bombard targets about twenty miles distant across battle lines and destroy enemy artillery positions and transport lines. These large guns would have to be properly mounted on concrete foundations. When a shell was fired, it would first make a large depression on the spot where it fell, and it would then bounce back in the air to explode with a great bang. When it exploded, thousands of small fragments would be dispersed with such great force in all directions that nobody or nothing in its vicinity could survive. It so happened that frequently these shells were wasted and did not result in any casualties, but every so often, it could blow up fifty people to smithereens at one go. Even a small fragment, about half a finger long, from this explosion was enough to bring down a man. A single fragment, hot as an ember, could cut through your boots or clothes and enter your body like a bullet. We saw many of these heavy artillery guns when we were marching forward; we also saw the tractors that were used to move them, instead of the usual horses. Adjacent to the guns was a contraption by which the heavy shells would be lifted up and inserted into the mouths of the guns. The men who worked these guns would have to wear protective earmuffs. When the gun was about to be fired, except for the man who did the firing, all the others would move away from it as there was always a chance that the gun would backfire and pulverize everyone around it. As this happened quite frequently, precautions were always taken in case the gun backfired. Besides the huge guns, there were other kinds of artillery that were used in this terrible war. The small sixteen- and eighteen-pounders were also very effective. These guns were used for routine everyday warfare, but they did pack a punch. These lightweight guns could be taken right up to the battlefront, and on occasions where a hand-to-hand combat was imminent, these guns could be used to neutralize enemy positions. Hundreds of such guns were lined up in front of the reserve trenches and were showering their destructive fire over enemy lines practically day and night. There were also the heavy 6-inch and 8-inch howitzers which were stationed behind our lines that fired on the enemy's communication lines and reserve trenches all through the day and caused a lot of destruction. They had an effective range of eight to ten miles and could destroy everything within their reach. The earth would tremble because of this incessant bombardment. Just as our guns were trained on the enemy, their guns would be trained on us and cause a lot of destruction. When these shells exploded, a strange type of foul-smelling black smoke would envelop the area.

Two Soldiers Cut in Half by a Shell

Let us now get back to our march. We started marching in the dead of night, and after traversing the deep craters caused by the shells, we finally reached the famous trenches of Match Wood at dawn. We now had to base ourselves in these trenches that had been dug into the earth. This was our first bitter experience of life in the trenches. Just as we were whispering among ourselves as to how we were going to stay here, the commanding officer ordered us to enter the trenches. Each company was assigned a different trench. We were then ordered to make our teas. Before we set out on this march, we had been given rations of tea and sugar. Each soldier had to make his own tea. Before we get on with the story, it would be useful to understand how these trenches were constructed. These trenches were similar to canals and were six feet deep and about three feet across. A man could conveniently walk about in an erect position in these trenches. Along the sides at short intervals, there were dugouts, small and cave-like, where men could shelter. As luck would have it, the dugouts in our trenches had not been dug deep enough. After we had our tea, we were ordered to start digging and deepening the dugouts. All of us set to work immediately. We were ordered to dig these dugouts as close to the base of the trenches as possible. If a shell landed anywhere near the trench, it could fall right through these dugouts and destroy everybody sheltering there. Once these dugouts were excavated, their roofs were lined with corrugated iron and pieces of wood to help them withstand these blasts. This was just the first night. We had not yet directly experienced enemy bombardment. In fact, we were rather keen to find out how it felt to be bombarded. After a day spent digging, we dragged our tired bodies into the dugouts and tried to get some sleep. Just then, an enemy shell exploded noisily in the vicinity. As the very first shell had exploded right next to where we were, all of us were terrorized. Its fragments embedded themselves in the upper walls of our trench. Just as we were wondering what to do next, a second shell landed behind our trench. We could hear heart-rending sounds from that area, but none of us had the courage to go out and investigate. Very soon shells began to explode everywhere. As we could hear the noise of each approaching shell, we would go crazy with fear, speculating where it would land. This heavy bombardment continued all through the night. We spent our very first night on the battlefields, enveloped by fright and dark thoughts, only to wake up to some shocking news. When we finally went to investigate the sounds we had heard the previous night, we discovered that two soldiers who had been sleeping in the trenches behind us had been completely pulverized by the shelling. We could not identify these unlucky soldiers as their badges had been destroyed. Their heads were lying far away from their torsos, and we could find no clues as to where their hands and legs lay buried in the rubble. The loss of these two courageous men before they saw any action spurred everyone to make their dugouts stronger. We spent the entire day in the trench out of sheer fear. There were hundreds of such trenches in the battlefield and each had been given a different name. Roads and alleys had been dug, connecting these trenches at the same level, and you could walk for miles along them. These trenches were named after London streets; our trench was named Liverpool Street. Once we entered these trenches, we had to cook for ourselves. In the morning, I made tea with the help of a companion; we had some 'dog biscuits' with us, which we soaked in water, then added a little sugar to it, and heated the mixture to make a sort of pudding. We filled our stomachs with this grub, topped it up with tea, and went for a stroll in this famous forest. At one time, these forests had provided an income of millions of rupees but had been completely destroyed by the bombing. All that was left were stumps of grand old trees. The area was strewn with thousands of objects—broken guns, bayonets, shovels, sickles, torn clothes of German soldiers and what not. I picked up a blue overcoat, once the possession of a German officer, and used it as a blanket. As this had been the site of a bloody hand-to-hand combat some time back, hands and legs were lying all around. Right behind our trenches were lined a series of artillery guns which had their barrels pointing towards the enemy. One after the other, they would fire 'Bang! Bang!' all through the day. We were also equally harassed by the enemy gunfire. This very first experience of action made a deep impression on our minds. Injured soldiers in the thousands thronged the dressing station near our trenches. The station was manned by the brave members of the Royal Army Medical Corps, and the courageous nurses worked hard day and night to serve the injured. It was an impressive sight to see ladies in military uniform driving the ambulance motor cars to transport the injured soldiers. Even as the German bombardment continued in the area, the ambulances would keep coming and going. It was only by God's grace that they were not hit.

Digging at Midnight

Orders to advance forward were suddenly issued at three o'clock in the night. We had to reluctantly abandon our dugouts which we had taken a lot of effort to make comfortable and advance along the support lines. After a march of five hours along a maze of trenches, we were issued orders to stop at a trench named Blackwater. Our platoon was supposed to relieve one of the Scottish Rifles. A platoon would be relieved after a stay of eight days in the support lines and the dangerous positions would be manned by a fresh platoon. We were not supposed to fight the Germans from this position, but were expected to dig new trenches in the dark of the night. Two companies would set out every night at eight with spades and shovels on their shoulders to work on the new trench lines at High Wood for four hours. After resting for four hours, they would set out on a march of five miles to bring water. Even this work of four hours every day was too strenuous for many of the men.

Poisonous Gas at Night

It was about ten in the night. We had been busy gathering our equipment to go on our assignment when the patrol on duty set off an emergency alarm. The minute this alarm was sounded, the entire encampment was aflutter with activity. There was not a second to be lost. Even the slightest delay could endanger the lives of the entire platoon as the enemy had fired grenades filled with poisonous gas. When these grenades exploded, noxious gas would diffuse all over the camp without any warning whatsoever. A single breath of this poison gas meant instantaneous death! The second the alarm for the poison gas was sounded, we had to wear specially medicated gas masks over our faces which would neutralize the effect of the gases. These gas masks were particularly tiresome to wear and they had to be kept on for hours on end. We also had to work all through the night with these gas masks covering our faces. The medication in the masks dried up our throats, besides making us feel nauseated. A rubber tube had been provided for breathing, which had to be kept inserted in the mouth. One could see through the glass provided in front of the eyes in these masks. A few of our companions died during this poison gas attack. They could not work with the masks over their faces as their breathing was stifled, and they pulled their masks off. The poison gas had pervaded the atmosphere, and we could see its effects on them as the poor fellows dropped dead after suffering for a few seconds. We were rendered absolutely helpless by this dastardly poison gas. Since we could never tell when a poison gas attack would be launched, we would always have to keep our gas masks in readiness as if our whole lives depended on them, especially at night. These grenades would also break like ordinary shells when they hit the ground. The only difference was that they would not explode on landing, and this would let us know it was a poison gas attack. It would first smell like pineapple and then the poison gas would spread rapidly. If you inhaled it for a couple of seconds, you would feel like you were being strangled, you would then foam at the mouth and suffer agonizing pain for a short while before you died. Thousands of soldiers died torturous deaths due to these poison gas attacks, but work was never suspended because of them. To prevent the enemy from advancing towards our trenches during these attacks, barbed wire would be stretched in front of the trenches to prevent sudden attacks. The laying of barbed wire was very hard work. First they would have to be carried over a distance of five miles. When they were being installed, soldiers would have to be in position to provide fire cover to the team. If the enemy discovered our movements, they would mount an artillery attack immediately. Both the sides used torches to observe the movements of the enemy in the dark of the night. There were many other kinds of lights, each of which had a different meaning. If only a single red light flashed in the sky, it meant the line was under threat. One green and one red light meant the commanding officer of the first line wanted the cover of artillery fire. Two red lights meant the enemy had attacked the first line of trenches while two green flashes meant artillery fire was to cease. These flashes of lights had different meanings which were coded. All through the night, the sky would be studded with colourful flashes of light as if firecrackers were being burst. The codes would be changed periodically to confuse the enemy.

10

The Battle of the Somme

At last it was our turn to see action, something we had been waiting for with our eyes peeled. Some of the soldiers were very eager to see the Germans in person and flaunt their muscle power, while quite a few were most distressed by the orders to advance forward to the front lines. We were to participate in the Battle of the Somme, which has already achieved legendary status in the Great War.

The Role of the Indian Army

The Indian Army also took part in the Battle of the Somme. The Bengal Lancers advanced under heavy fire from the Germans right up to the German trenches and forced them to retreat. On this occasion, our platoon was ordered to advance to the firing line. Our undercover march started at about one o'clock in the night. We had been strictly warned not to utter a single word. With great difficulty, we managed to advance, digging a few trenches and walking all through the night, only to find ourselves in a very unfortunate position in the morning. A German observation balloon which had been flying above us had spotted us, and very soon our route came under heavy fire. Shells were exploding all around us. To escape them, we would lie flat on the ground for a short while before running to advance a little forward. A wave of fear rippled through our platoon. Soldiers were falling all around us with piteous shrieks, but there was nothing that could be done. Each man was on his own and could not be bothered about anybody else. Others would advance by stepping on those injured soldiers who had fallen to the ground. We had no option but to move forward. We also had no idea what kinds of difficulties we were to face as we advanced. Many of our men were lagging behind, but we could not wait for them, and at about twelve noon we reached the famous jungles of Del Ville Wood where we felt we could finally heave a sigh of relief. But fate had other things in store for us. There were no trenches beyond the next twenty-five yards from where we were located. We could not step out of the trenches as we would have been sitting ducks for German guns. The Germans were hardly at any distance from where we were—say about a hundred yards away in their trenches. In spite of this situation, the Commanding Officer gave orders to advance further. We had no option but to run, and we ran in pairs. We would advance about ten steps before throwing ourselves flat on the ground. Our progress did not last very long. Soon enough, the enemy started firing at us with their machine guns. We were staring death in the eye. But as luck would have it, there had been a fierce battle on this very site just four days ago, and the bodies of dead soldiers were lying all around us. These corpses proved very useful in sheltering us from the enemy gunfire. As we advanced, we would lie behind these corpses, and they would act as our shield taking all the gunfire. Ah, what a terrible experience! Just one bullet and we would also have joined the army of cold corpses!

War in the Skies

After a very desperate battle and the loss of over fifty soldiers, we were lucky enough to be able to take possession of the trenches. Because of the non-stop action during the night and the better part of the day, we had not even had a cup of tea, much less anything to eat. I had managed to eat a couple of biscuits while moving forward. This was all I had had, with which I had to be content for the whole day. Once we took possession of the trenches, the different companies of the platoon were immediately assigned positions. While the A and C Companies were assigned the forward trenches, the B Company was assigned the communication line, which was about ten yards behind us, and the D Company was a further fifteen yards behind them in the support line. We were immediately ordered to make structural improvements in the trenches, which meant more digging. These trenches were not deep enough for a man to stand erect. The soldiers were tired of standing with their backs bent for extended lengths of time. The trenches were also rather narrow and we could hardly move around in them. We began using our small shovels and spades, and started digging at a steady pace, making as little noise as possible. We had hardly started digging when the sky above us was criss-crossed by enemy planes. They had been sent to monitor our progress and signal our position. Soon enough, our lines were bombarded by their artillery positions and we had to suspend our digging operations. Before we go further ahead with our story, let us take a look at the role of these aeroplanes in the war.

These aerial barques would fly high over enemy camps and their trenches, and photograph our positions to determine where the enemy was concentrated and how their lines were positioned. They would then go back and relay all the information to the base. They were, however, most deadly when they worked in conjunction with the artillery. These planes would be assigned to specific batteries; during an assault, these planes would hover above the enemy lines and relay back information on where the shells were landing. If the shells were landing at too short or too long a distance from the enemy trenches, they would immediately ask the battery to adjust its range. If they spotted a shell that had landed at the right place, they would immediately signal a 'repeat fire' to completely pulverize the position. Sometimes they would come in huge numbers and we would be carpeted with aerial fire. These aerial barques completely terrorized everybody in the trenches. The minute they appeared above us, we would be ordered to remain as still as possible. If we froze in our positions, it was possible that they might not spot us. These planes were also mounted with machine guns that would merrily go 'Bang! Bang!' and wreak havoc on those below. Occasionally, planes from both the sides would engage each other in the skies, and this was indeed a sight to behold. To contain these demons of the skies, a different kind of specially designed artillery known as 'anti-aircraft guns' would be deployed. They would keep up a relentless fire on the planes from the minute they were spotted.

Storm on a Dark Night

This being our first day in the firing-line trenches, all the soldiers were not assigned specific duties. Some of them were free while others were stationed at specific locations on sentry duty in batches. As these trenches were not deep enough for the soldiers to stand erect and peep over them to monitor the enemy's movements, a special glass contraption was designed, which could be attached to the tip of the bayonet of one's gun. This helped the sentry sit down and monitor the space between our trenches and those of the enemy. At short intervals, they would slightly raise their guns very carefully, and peep into the glass and see if there were any enemy advances. Every so often, German snipers would shoot at the bayonets of these soldiers with perfect aim. These German snipers were a real nuisance. At night, snipers from both sides would emerge from the trenches and shoot at the slightest movement. Besides these man-made miseries, we also had to face the fury of nature. In addition to the relentless noise of heavy guns firing through the dark night, we had to brave the most frightful thunder accompanied by incessant rain. It would rain all through the night and the trenches would be flooded. We would be standing in chest-deep water, wondering when the enemy would mount a surprise attack. Even as our boots and clothes were weighed down by the squelching mud and water, our officers would keep braying at us: 'Beware! The enemy might attack!' Buffeted from all sides and terrorized by the incessant guns, there were many soldiers who felt it would be far better to emerge from the trenches and take a chance with the enemy gunfire. There were others who were so paralysed by fear that they would appear almost insane and would not stir from their positions. Even if they had to answer nature's call, they would be unable to take a single step. They would just dig a shallow hole right where they were and do their dirty business. In spite of their paralysis, they were somehow drafted to do some work by the booming orders of the officers. As mentioned earlier, the front line was manned by batches, each batch consisting of one sentry and five soldiers, with a non-commissioned officer in charge of them. They were responsible for holding the front line, and each soldier had to be on strict lookout for one hour at a time. A Lewis gun or a machine gun would be placed between every three batches. If the sentry felt that the enemy was trying to make an advance or if there was the slightest movement detected in the enemy lines, the guns would start firing. These Lewis guns played a very important role in this devastating war. These lightweight guns weighed only twenty-nine pounds and could be easily handled by one man who could move it from place to place, and when ordered, start firing at the rate of four hundred bullets per minute. Each of these guns was equivalent to a hundred rifles. We always had to be prepared at the firing line with all these arrangements.

Tear-Inducing Chilli Bombs

After spending a miserable night in the trenches, we were shivering in our wet clothes in the morning. Suddenly we were ordered to 'Stand to!' Now what was this for? Even as we were wondering what it was all about, a gas that felt like chillies began pervading the trenches. Shrill orders to wear our goggles were urgently issued. When the gas first attacked us, we could hardly understand what was happening. The gas began to envelop us from every direction and gas shells lobbed from the enemy lines were silently exploding all around us. Our eyes were in a state of extreme irritation. It felt as if they would burst. We could hardly see anything; tears were flowing freely from our eyes, and it felt dark and terrifying. In spite of all this, everybody got into fighting position, facing the enemy lines and waiting for the inevitable attack. It was generally understood that the enemy released this gas just before it launched an attack. It rendered our soldiers blind and immobile for a brief while, and during this period, they could get the better of us and wrest our trenches. We could hardly open our eyes since the chilli gas had caused our eyes to turn red and swell up. How was a soldier to fight under such adverse circumstances? Along with this chilli gas, regular artillery fire was also kept up by the enemy, which further exacerbated the situation. To combat the nuisance of these 'tear shells' and to protect the eyes, a special kind of protective spectacles had been designed. They were made of ordinary glass through which everything could be seen, and the frame was fringed with flannel which ensured that the gas did not make contact with the eyes. The only saving grace was that exposure to tear gas, unlike poison gas, was not fatal; it merely left you blind for a short while.

On a Starvation Diet

Besides all the problems described above, we had yet another major problem to contend with: how to silence our hunger pangs. Soldiers on the firing line had to remain awake day and night and had no chance to lie down. To make matters worse, they had to scrounge for food. Admittedly, there was a lot of food dumped beyond the support lines as the motor transport guys would weave through the heaviest artillery fire to supply the food. Transporting the food from the dump to the firing lines was a major challenge for the soldiers. They would step out in large numbers to bring the food stuffed in small gunny bags back from the dump to the front line. The extreme conditions in the trenches, what with them being flooded with rainwater and slush, and the incessant firing of the enemy many a time prevented them from returning safely. They would be injured and fall down en route, and the food would also lie rotting there. The situation at the firing line was indeed desperate. The D Company had been assigned the support line and was responsible for supplying us with food, but as they came under heavy fire, they could not venture out of their trenches. Even though we were at the very front, the lines immediately to our rear suffered the most, bearing the brunt of the artillery fire. At least fifteen to twenty men from one company would get injured every day, and the condition of the injured was indeed very pitiable. How was food to reach us under this situation? We had to subsist on the few packets of biscuits and bully beef we had carried with us. Where was the question of getting a hot cup of tea? Not a single wisp of smoke was supposed to escape from the trenches. If the enemy spotted smoke coming from a trench, they would consider it to be a live target and fire immediately. The poor soldiers would go scrounging around for cigarette stubs. Such was the dire situation at the front lines–starvation, mud and slush–and the relentless artillery fire had so harassed the soldiers that they were a pathetic sight to behold. They had not shaved for days. How do you think they looked? It is best left to the imagination!

Our Final Assault

This was to be our last day at the famous Del Ville Wood. After many days of suffering and troubles, would it be too much to say that our imminent relief seemed like a new lease of life to us? Early in the morning, the news had already spread in the trenches that we were to be relieved tonight; our faces were aglow with delight. Just after noon, more authoritative news reached us, which was slightly different. We were indeed to be relieved, but we would have to perform some more arduous tasks tonight; the soldiers welcomed this news as a means of getting out of the trenches. All of us had been eagerly looking forward to being relieved for many days. Instead of spending yet another day in the slushy trenches, it was more preferable to emerge from them and show our courage in hand-to-hand combat. As per the orders issued to us, we were to launch our attack at ten in the night. Two companies were to lead the attack while the other two companies were to support us in the assault, and the trenches which we were to evacuate were to be occupied by the 4th Suffolk Regiment. All preparations had been made for a full-on artillery assault at the same time. Some of the soldiers were eagerly looking forward to the hour of the assault, while the colour had drained out of the faces of others.

This supposedly minor assault was sure to claim the lives of many soldiers, but nobody knew who it would be. As things turned out, luck was on our side on this dark and evil night. It was pitch dark and the rain was falling steadily, and the roads were so slushy that they were of a porridge-like consistency. The enemy might have felt that there was very little likelihood of an attack from us in such awful weather. Our strategy was to attack under the cover of bad weather. Every minute seemed like an hour. As we waited, we could hear our hearts beating within our chests. After a seemingly eternal wait, it was finally the dark hour when we were to launch our attack. Just as orders were barked out to get us ready for the final assault, a volley of artillery fire passed over our heads towards the enemy lines. Within the blink of an eye, the Germans returned fire. Hundreds of shells were exploding loudly all around us. Their smoke darkened the skies, and we were already so scared that any enthusiasm we might have had for escaping from the trenches evaporated. Before we could think any further, orders were screamed out: 'Over the top! Best to luck!' The minute we heard the orders, we jumped out of the trenches and emerged into the open. We could soon hear the plaintive screams of our fellow soldiers, many of whom had fallen victim to the fire from the mortars and the machine guns. The rest of us braves, mindless of the fate of our colleagues, kept advancing. Lying flat on the ground, we crawled for over an hour and were lucky enough to finally make it to the enemy front lines. We then lobbed small bombs into their trenches and soon jumped into the trenches for a face-to-face duel. At this stage, many soldiers lost their lives to close-range enemy bullets, while some were bayoneted to death. We were able to take ten prisoners and capture one machine gun. We were about to turn back but heavy enemy artillery fire prevented us from doing so. This was the heaviest bombardment I had ever seen, with thousands of shells exploding simultaneously all around us. Because of the rain, mud and slush, our clothes felt like they weighed a ton. Dragging all this paraphernalia with us, a few of us were lucky enough to get back to our lines. Even as we were luxuriating in our good fortune, Lady Luck finally deserted us. A heavy shell landed just ten yards from where we were and exploded very loudly; we tried to jump away from it, but were not lucky enough to escape without being hit. I was also hit by a fragment. Even though I jumped as quickly as I could into a trench, my leg was injured in a gruesome manner. This had to happen just on the very last day when we were about to be relieved from trench duty. When fate turns against you, there is nothing you can do!

Adding Insult to Injury

Like me, there were hundreds of injured soldiers moaning and lying unattended in the trenches. There was nobody to listen to our groans or pay any attention to us. Our troubles were just starting. If you managed to reach the dressing station, your troubles could come to an end. But in this bloody battle, it seemed like an impossibility. It was routine for hundreds of soldiers to get injured every day, and each platoon had its own stretcher-bearers who were supported by men from the Royal Army Medical Corps. For this assault, special working parties had also been formed. The firing and the destruction was, however, so severe that all these arrangements came to nought. Unlucky soldiers with stomach or leg injuries would frequently die a painful death in the trenches. If an injured soldier managed to drag himself away from the action, he stood a better chance of survival. Once you reached the dressing station, you would be one among thousands of injured soldiers crying for medical attention. The best possible care was given to them. There would be trolleys and vehicles from the Ambulance Corps to take them to the casualty clearing station. Once you reached this location, you could safely assume that your troubles had come to an end. All it needed was a cup of hot tea to make the injured soldier feel much better. After the seemingly endless days of nightmarish existence starving in the trenches, a cup of tea and the ministrations of female nurses felt like heaven. And then it was 'Back for Blighty!'

11

Back for Blighty

If a soldier got injured in the war, he was well taken care of. Once he reached the dressing station, all his problems seemed to come to an end. During a battle, numerous such dressing stations were erected at various locations, and they were serially numbered. Besides, there was a casualty clearing station in the reserve lines, generally referred to as the CCS. Grievously injured soldiers were transported to hospitals from the CCS. In accordance with these rules, I was also laid on a stretcher and loaded on to an ambulance car and had to bid goodbye to the battlegrounds of the Somme. I was taken to the famous French city of Rouen, where I was admitted into Hospital No. 5. The feverish activities in the hospital were a sight to behold. When I reached the hospital at nine o'clock in the night, it was pitch dark. I was delicately lifted from my stretcher and placed on a comfortable bed. My uniform, in complete tatters after many days in the trenches, was stripped off me and I was given a kerosene bath. This was done so that the vermin that stuck to my body were completely killed off. After a spell in the trenches, our bodies were covered with white vermin. Our skin was infected and scabby, and had to be completely disinfected with kerosene. As it had been days since we had even washed our faces, much less taken a proper bath or shower, this dry bath was indeed a benediction. Anything we desired was immediately proffered. The European doctors passed by on their rounds twice at night, while the nurses were always at hand to attend to our littlest needs. After spending a week or so at the hospital in Rouen, it was decided that I would be transferred back to England. The Red Cross train dropped us off at a new station erected opposite the docks at Le Havre. All through the journey, the French populace greeted us with bouquets of flowers and baskets of fruits. We were objects of adulation at every station where the train halted. At Le Havre, the Red Cross steamer was waiting for us. I was very delicately transferred from my stretcher to a bed, and was once again ready to inhale the salty air of the sea. We were now under the care of the Royal Army Medical Corps. When we reached Southampton, there was yet another Red Cross train waiting for us. At about six in the evening, it left Southampton to take us to South Wales, where we were deboarded at Whitchurch, a small village near the famous city of Cardiff. Ambulances were waiting at the station to transfer us to the big hospital in Whitchurch. The local populace thronged the station and the entire route to get a sight of the brave soldiers who had injured themselves fighting for the nation. As our ambulance made its way to the hospital, cries of 'Hurray!' rent the skies as multicoloured kerchiefs were tossed into the air. We made our way through this tumultuous welcome to finally reach the magnificent receiving hall at the hospital. As soon as our stretchers entered the hall, we were offered beef tea and biscuits in the manner of children spoilt silly. In short, everybody was most eager to serve us in every way possible. The injured soldiers were allocated to different wards, and I was taken to the F-2 ward on the first floor, where a comfortable mattress awaited me.

Wartime Hospital and the Company of Ladies

During the war, everybody at home was eager to be of any kind of service to soldiers who had returned injured from the various theatres of war. Instead of being bombarded by exploding shells, we were now spending our days being entertained by the sweet voices of the nurses. The hospital had a capacity to house about one thousand injured soldiers. The doctors and nurses who had volunteered for this national service took a lot of care and effort to keep such a large number happy and occupied. Besides, high-class ladies from local families were equally keen to keep us entertained. They would bring us baskets full of cake, biscuits, cigarettes and other delicious stuff. Soldiers who could not walk about were fed at their beds. Those who were mobile were constantly being invited for tea to various places. During the afternoons, when the soldiers were allowed to leave the hospital for a while, our new friends, these ladies, would be waiting outside the gates in their motor cars. Besides them, there were other groups of ladies who would be loitering outside the hospital gates nearly an hour before visiting time, eagerly awaiting their soldier friends. It was as if they were duty-bound to keep the injured soldiers in the best of spirits. Many of the activities within the hospital were also managed by the high-class ladies who had taken it upon themselves to organize dances and dramas for the soldiers. As per the rules of this hospital, soldiers could leave the premises between one and five in the afternoon. Injured soldiers in uniform were entitled to free tea and refreshments at the special YMCA set up for them in the city, with facilities for various kinds of games and sports. Each day would bring us in contact with ladies from different neighbourhoods. As the war continued to prolong month after month, and the number of casualties and injured soldiers began to explode, these ladies worked themselves up into a fright. Many ladies who had not been keen on getting married before the war were now in such a disturbed state that they were most eager to tie the knot. Everybody felt that marriage during the war was an honourable deed, indeed an obligation. This craziness assumed such gross proportions that couples would get married merely after a day's acquaintance, either in the hospital or outside.

Wartime London

I experienced the hospitality of these beautiful Welsh people for three months, during which time I completely recovered from all my injuries. It was as if I was born again. On discharge, decked up in army uniform and carrying a newly issued kitbag, I found myself at Cardiff station waiting for a train to London to spend fifteen days of 'sick leave'. I was looking forward to enjoying the urban pleasures of London. During the war, large buildings and hotels had been requisitioned through the medium of the YMCA for soldiers who were passing through. Besides, new buildings had been erected near stations so that soldiers arriving in the middle of the night could easily find places to sleep. All these facilities were provided at very cheap rates: sixpence a night per soldier for a bed to sleep in. At large stations, soldiers were given tea and snacks for free. If one were to say that everything was designed for the comfort of the soldiers, it would not be an exaggeration. The rest of the population had a hard time of it. Food was always a problem, and even buying a pound of potatoes was a struggle. If potatoes had to be bought, women and children with their small baskets would queue up from five in the morning at the potato vendor's shop. Would it be an exaggeration to say that this line extended for over a mile? As the day progressed, the queue would lengthen instead of shortening, and with all the activity, it would seem as if it was a fair. It is unlikely that England had ever before seen such scenes. People would queue up without even having had a cup of tea or breakfast, in the hope that they might lay their hands on a small quantity of potatoes; but evening would see them return empty-handed. Often the stock of potatoes would run out, even though they were strictly rationed—only one pound per family. As the war intensified, many people uprooted their flower beds and planted potatoes. Wherever one looked, potatoes were being planted. Besides the shortage of potatoes, there was also a great shortage of sugar. Sugar was strictly rationed and sold only against coupons. Each person was allotted a pound of sugar per week. Even if one had money, one could not buy more sugar than this quantity. If one went to have a cup of tea at a hotel or restaurant, it would be futile to expect sugar; instead, a sachet or two of saccharine would be provided. Many would carry their sugar rations along with them when they went out. How could they do without their sweet cup of tea? Sugar had a more important place in their purses than money. There were shortages of butter, bread, meat, and practically everything else. It was as if the demons of famine and drought had taken it upon themselves to shower misfortune over this beautiful city.

Theatres in Desolate London

After having spent some time in the European theatre of war, I had thought that, once I returned to London, I would also have fun in the famous theatres of London. There are very few cities in the world where the craze for the theatre and the cinematograph is as widespread as in London. You would be surprised to note that in the pre-war days, if you intended to go to the theatre on a Saturday, tickets had to be booked three or four days in advance if you wanted to be assured of a seat. If you wanted to catch a performance without reserving your ticket, you would have to queue up three to four hours in advance outside the theatre. The queues would be so long that the theatre itself would not be visible from the end of the line. Don't these people get tired of queuing up? I always used to wonder whether this kind of queue formed outside only one or two theatres? But no, these long lines could be seen outside practically every theatre. In spite of the crowds, there would hardly be any pushing around. Everybody would be standing peacefully, awaiting their turn. Quite likely, many of them would not get a ticket for the show. Such was the discipline in this country. However, during the war, it was as if they had launched a non-cooperation movement against these theatres. The theatres were desolate and empty. The ladies of London were now keen on national service; instead of enjoying themselves at the theatre, they preferred to work the night shift in ammunition factories. And the gentlemen who had escorted them to these theatres were themselves actors in a different kind of theatre–the theatre of war. They were daily enacting new roles and trying to dodge the bullets of the enemy all through the night. How was a poor soul like me going to have fun in the theatres of wartime London?

The End of Fashion

You may not believe it, but it seemed like the desolation of the theatres also seemed to signify an end of fashion as it was known in pre-war London. Shops which used to cater to the latest fashion had to down their shutters. Women had bid a final adieu to expensive evening dresses. Even young girls seemed to prefer army uniforms. There was a craze among fashionable ladies to appear in khaki in public, and they were proud of it. They would dress themselves up in khaki cloth, crop their long tresses very short, and preen about twirling a baton. Some of the more forward girls began to make the most of this new-found freedom. You could see groups of girls enjoying themselves with glasses of beer in their hands at public drinking houses, with lit cigarettes drooping from their lips. The population suddenly found that many of the old restrictions had disappeared, and this new-found freedom put the famous city of London in a very delicate situation.

The World-Famous Hyde Park

In those battle-weary days, practically everything in London was being destroyed. Is it then surprising that the famous parks of London presented a desolate sight to visitors? Many of our Indian tourists who have been to London are surely familiar with Hyde Park. If not for this large park which extends for miles, Londoners would have gone crazy. As evening falls, people are drawn to this park as if by magnets. The colourful dresses, the song and dance, and the fun present a very different atmosphere. People just cannot get enough of it; after having heard the king's own band in the evening, they still want more! The ambience of this park gets transformed by the activities of the night. During the pre-war days, tourists from various countries visited this park, but when I visited it during the war, things were very different. The seven gigantic iron gates of this world-famous park and the fences seemed to have acquired a rusty look. Instead of angelic ladies gadding about, there was a lot of military activity. It had become the headquarters of motor transport and there was a constant traffic of motor lorries. The noise and clamour presented a very different scenario. The nearby Regent's Park also presented a similar scene; the handsome benches of the municipality seemed to have been completely deserted by its denizens. The courageous ladies of the NAD were busy washing and cleaning for the war effort, leaving London completely desolate.

Nature's Fury and Aerial Bombing

The one and only reason for the complete desolation and destruction of London was the war. The regular bombing of London by the flying barques had created an atmosphere of terror in the city. The only objective of the enemy was to target London and wreak havoc so that the population was terrorized. And they seemed to have succeeded to a large extent. Under the cover of night, these planes would assemble in large numbers to shower bombs over London. When the alarm for an air attack was sounded, people would run helter-skelter trying to find shelter. One of the main reasons people did not move about at night was these avian demons. They would stay in their houses and bury themselves in their cellars. The situation of women and children during these air raids was very pitiable. If people were walking about on roads when the Zeppelin alarms were sounded, they would run into the nearest underground station to take refuge. These stations would be overflowing with crowds. People preferred to travel by underground trains rather than by trams or omnibuses because they felt safer. Large buildings would come crumbling down in front of one's eyes during these attacks. Many people, including children, lost their lives during these attacks. The entire city of London would tremble and quiver during the bombardment. Even as these aerial bombings demoralized the population, nature vent its fury on the city. There were great changes in the weather patterns. The heavy and unrelenting artillery bombing in France drove the clouds across the Channel to England, and there was incessant rain in London. It was as if it would never stop. The famous yellow fog of London was also on the ascendancy during this time. It had the city in its grip all through the day and night. Even a newly erected building would soon acquire a dark hue. As the labouring classes of London had gone off to fight the war, there was hardly any maintenance or painting done during the war. The roads were also in a bad condition. The once-famous electric street lights of the London municipality had been painted black and were a miserable sight to behold.

The Female Police of London

London had been reduced to a shadow of its pre-war magnificence by the aerial bombings and other calamities. If it had to suffer attacks on a daily basis, did it not need a rescue team? We are all aware of the pre-war prestige of the London policemen, who are known as bobbies. A mere wiggling of a finger by a bobby was enough to stop a rich gentleman in his tracks. It is said that one had to give an examination to enrol even as an ordinary constable. They had to have the entire map of London impressed on their minds. If you were to ask a bobby for directions, he would give you the most exact directions to get to your destination by the shortest route, not missing a single turn, and also reel off the numbers of the trams and omnibuses which went in that direction. There is no likelihood of getting lost in London. Owners of large firms and businesses and rich men are able to get a good night's sleep because of the watchfulness of these bobbies. The policeman on the night shift would periodically check the locks of all the shops and premises on his beat. If a new man were to take over the beat, they would jointly check all the locks before charge was handed over. The new bobby would then be responsible for the beat. But this war did not leave even these policemen alone, and they were also sucked into it. They had to join the war effort and shoulder guns. This obviously led to a severe shortage of policemen in London. These vacancies were filled by the erstwhile fashionable ladies of the city who did not shy away from sporting the helmet of the police constables. These ladies, who at one time used to parade in the latest fashion and strut about in high heels, presented a strange sight patrolling the streets of London with their police uniforms and heavy boots.

Back to the War

I was depressed by the sights of London ravaged by war. My dreams of having a good time there had turned into a nightmare. I had utterly wasted my ten days of leave in the city. Rarely does one get this kind of leave in the army. Only when a soldier has recovered from injuries sustained during the war is he entitled to this leave. He would also get a free railway ticket, and besides his pay, a daily allowance of two shillings and sixpence to be able to stay in a place of his choice and recover his strength so that he was ready to fight again in the war. It was on this principle that I had been granted leave. I had built many castles in the air about my holiday, but all of them came crashing down when I reached London. And now it was time to rejoin my regiment which was then in Chatham. I was ordered to join the 5th Middlesex Battalion. Chatham is a three- or four-hour train ride from London and it did not take me very long to get there. Chatham was a major centre for the navy and now it had a big army encampment too. New soldiers were being trained in this camp before being sent off to the war. I also received two months of fresh training in this camp, and finally one day was ordered to proceed to Egypt, a place I had never ever imagined I would visit. It was back to the old routine: off to the quartermaster stores where we had to assemble our kits to suit the fighting fields of Egypt. After an inspection by the commanding officer, we were off to Gillingham station to catch a train to Southampton via London. From Southampton we reached the famous port of Marseilles, where the steamer *Saxon* was belching smoke from its chimney as it waited for us.

THE MIDDLE EASTERN FRONT

12
Off to Egypt

Belching dark smoke from its chimneys, the *Saxon* moved away from the coast of France with about five thousand soldiers as passengers. All of them were headed towards the battlefields of Egypt.

A Japanese Escort

During times of war, if a ship carrying five thousand soldiers did not reach its destination safely, it would be considered a major setback to the English war effort. It had been heard from various quarters that German submarines were wreaking havoc at sea. We were all on tenterhooks. But thanks to the short-statured Japanese, we were being fully protected during this journey. The Japanese had sent two of their destroyer ships to escort us; there was one ahead of us, leading the way, while the other brought up the rear. On the very second day, in the afternoon, just as we were having lunch, we heard artillery fire from these destroyers. Soon enough, we were on the edge of our seats. All of us abandoned our meal midway and ran outside to investigate the cause of this new trouble. We soon heard that a German submarine had come too close for comfort and the Japanese barque had had to open fire and was apparently successful in destroying the submarine. In spite of the presence of these Japanese destroyers, we had to be very careful ourselves. We had to be on watch during the entire journey. Watches were assigned all through the night and the day. Armed sentries were posted at short distances along the deck of the steamer. Our sailing boats, which were normally berthed on deck, were always kept hanging from their cords, ready to be launched if necessary. These vessels were also guarded by armed sentries. The ever-present danger of submarines necessitated all these measures. In preparation for any emergency situations (God spare us!), soldiers were taught special drills on the steamer. Each soldier was made aware of the locations of the small life rafts and the assembly points in the event of an emergency. If the short piercing whistle of the ship was sounded, we were to come as we were and immediately assemble in front of our assigned life rafts. We were particularly instructed not to stop to collect even a single item. Each soldier had been given a lifebelt when he boarded the ship. He had to wear it all through the day, and it had to be kept close at hand even while sleeping at night. If a soldier or even an officer was ever found not wearing a belt, the punishment was very severe. Smoking on deck or even lighting any kind of flame was strictly prohibited. Lights that could be seen from outside of the steamer were also not allowed. These precautions had to be taken at night to prevent detection by the submarines. These submarines were practically invisible in the dark waters of the night and they could slip past even the strictest watch. After having spent many tension-filled days and nights, shouts of joy were heard as we finally spotted the famous Egyptian port of Alexandria. Our caretaker destroyer ships moved aside, and both the steamers gave a final salute to them. Shouts of 'Hurray!' rent the air as the English soldiers expressed their gratitude to the Japanese for their services. For about ten minutes, the celebrations continued, and the coast of Egypt seemed to reverberate with the noise and the fanfare. I can never forget the impression this scene made on me.

On the Bloody Battlefields of the Crusades

I consider myself extremely lucky that I managed to return alive from the killing fields of France and have been able to share my experiences and the trauma of that stint. And having returned alive from France, my new experiences have provided me with an opportunity to relate the injustice done to the Indian and white armies in Egypt and Mesopotamia. Soldiers who return after a stint on the Western Front are under the impression there are no other battlefields except those in France; but my personal experience in Egypt gives the lie to this impression. I am now going to narrate how the brave soldiers confronted nature in all its fury in Egypt and Mesopotamia. The battlefields of the Crusades are unknown to none. The extensive deserts and the mountain peaks have seen many a great battle over the centuries, and they continue to keep guard over this country and challenge new armies. History tells us that in the year 1799, the powerful army of the great Napoleon Bonaparte traversed these very deserts, but he could not capture the holy city of Jerusalem.

In Alexandria, we were encamped at the large military camp called Mustafa Camp. We were provided with our entire weaponry and kitbag here, carrying which we marched towards the station at night to catch a train for the battlefields. A special train was ready and waiting for us soldiers. We flopped down wherever space was available. Letting out a volley of shrieks from its whistle, the train gathered speed to gallop like a rhinoceros over the tracks. This railway line runs along the Suez Canal and extends up to Port Said in one direction, while it branches off to Cairo on the other. We were, however, to get down midway at Al-Cantara, an important station on the Suez Canal. From here we were to march towards our destination. When we finally reached our camp, we saw a line of tents, about fifty of them, erected on the sands. There was nothing else to be seen: sand, sand, and more sand!

Wire-Mesh Roads on Desert Sand

The first thing that put us off at Al-Cantara was the sand. Since this was our first experience of desert sand, we could hardly walk on it and would sink up to our ankles. It seemed as if we had forgotten how to walk. We are walking as if we were babies learning to take our first steps. If we could barely walk, how were we to fight on these desert sands, we wondered. Luckily, we soon heard that we were to be provided with eight days of training at Al-Cantara on how to walk on these sands before being sent to the front lines. Our regiment was encamped on the front lines about a few miles from where we were, but we were detained here. Instead of fighting, it was back to the old shovel-and-spade routine for us. A new railway line was being built from Al-Cantara over these sands, and thousands of soldiers had been drafted to build it. Before the railway lines could be laid, a proper road had to be built, which was hard work. There was an acute shortage of water and the fine sand made things very difficult. How was a road to be built? The solution was to lay a double layer of wire mesh over the sand so that a firm surface could be obtained. Even this work had to be done by the poor soldiers.

Hard March over Desert Sand

It was finally our turn. We were already a frightened lot after spending a few days at Al-Cantara. But the time had now arrived when we had some very good reasons to be afraid. When we were issued orders to march further ahead to the front line, we had to pack up each and every one of our belongings and assemble on the grounds awaiting further orders. Besides our usual equipment and luggage, we were also issued a bebeset, that is, two pieces of a rather thick cloth and a wooden pole. These two sheets of cloth could be hung on the pole to form a small tent that could be used for shelter. Two soldiers could be accommodated in this tent. Once all this luggage had been mounted on our shoulders, we were ready to march. We were to join our battalion, which, if rumours were to be believed, was encamped at various spots in Al-Rafa. Before we could get to Rafa, we had to cross the terrorizing sand dunes. It was obvious from the very start that it was going to be a very tiring walk for the soldiers. We could not get a sure footing in the sand, and often our legs would sink deep into it. Wherever we looked, all we could see was white sand, sand, and yet more sand; besides sand, there was nothing to be seen! Added to this, we had a donkey's load on our backs; things could not get any worse. The hard march meant that soldiers had to help each other constantly. A hot wind would hammer the fine sand particles on to our body and cause a lot of pain. Our eyes were burning red, and God alone knew how much sand we had ingested even as we breathed. And our faces had become so dark that it seemed like we had just stepped out of our graves. In spite of all this trauma, many of the mischievous British Tommies were still up for some fun and ribbing. If we were to go looking for a wife in this condition, what would the poor girl have to say about us? Surely there must be a lady somewhere who would fall for our handsome faces? As per army regulations, we were allowed to rest periodically and have some tea and water, but the sand continued to annoy us even then. I am sure a lot of sand got into our food, but we just amused ourselves by considering it as garnish. If by chance any object was left out in the open, it would soon be covered with sand and be lost. The power and fury of nature is enough to make a man crazy. When we had traversed this stretch of fifty or sixty miles of sand and reached the sea at Al-Arish, our faces bloomed with joy on seeing the water. As this desert is adjacent to the Mediterranean Sea, it provided great relief to the soldiers once we got there. The water was very shallow in these parts and not even a small boat could enter this area. We, however, flopped in the water like buffaloes and tried to wash the sand off our bodies and enjoyed ourselves thoroughly. There was nothing to see in Al-Arish. On one side was the sea, and on the other, the desert stretched ahead for miles. Baldwin I of Jerusalem died here in the year 1118, and a small tomb buffeted by sand can still be seen. As the war progressed, the face of Al-Arish changed completely. Since its air is very invigorating, the Australians constructed a huge hospital there. A new double railway line has been laid, which passes between the sea and the hospital there. This silent place certainly deserves all the current prosperity it is experiencing. It is the working of the wheel of fate. What attracted my attention the most was the presence of a number of date trees. When I saw them, I could hardly hold back the tears from my eyes as they reminded me of my old dear town of Navsari and its palm trees and toddy.

13

Desert Battles

Finally we managed to reach the encampment of our new battalion—the Second 10th Middlesex. They were cowering in a corner trying to avoid the gaze of the enemy. We could hardly make out the encampment from a distance, since the entire army was hiding in holes dug in the ground in the form of caves. Even the small tents had been dipped in dirt and mud to camouflage them. If an enemy aircraft flew by overhead, it would be difficult for them to identify it as a camp. When our new group joined the camp, the old hands frightened us out of our wits by informing us that a large number of enemy planes flew by every morning to bomb the encampment. We were already in a state of terror, and this new bit of information only made things worse. The other recruits who had come with me had absolutely no fighting experience. They had just joined fresh, and these initial experiences were enough to scare them. To make matters worse, we were assigned patrol duty on the very night we arrived. Nobody was really bothered about the number of miles we had trekked to get there or the fact that most of the new arrivals had no fighting experience!

Encampment in the Desert

Our camp was erected on a sandy desert. The war in Egypt was completely different from the one in France. When we engaged the enemy in France, we dug trenches and established our positions, but similar trenches could not be dug in Egypt. It was very difficult to dig trenches in the desert sand, and therefore, a very different strategy was employed here. Sand was filled in small gunny sacks, and these sacks were piled one upon another to form a circular wall which would form a defensive position. On the outside, barbed wire would be piled all around it to reinforce the defence. The barbed wire would be laid about five to seven feet deep, so an enemy could not attack our positions suddenly without having cast aside the barbed wire. This position was known as an outpost. During the night, they would be manned by soldiers, who ensured that the enemy did not launch a sudden attack. During the day, our cavalry would send out patrols to monitor enemy positions. In this theatre of war, the enemy positions could be thousands of feet away from our front lines, unlike those in France, where the enemy trenches were practically adjacent to ours. The assault was generally launched by the cavalry or the Camel Corps who provided a clear route for the infantry. The foot soldiers did not have to fight it out alone in this area.

Beersheba–the Strongest Fortification in Palestine

In this desert battle, we always advanced in the company of the cavalry, but the time had now come for us to show our prowess. Numerous battles were fought in the sands of Egypt–we won some and we lost some–but at length we had managed to advance to the gates of Palestine where many fierce battles were being fought. This place was known as Beersheba and it was a very strategic location;

at this point, thousands of miles of desert gave way to a chain of hills and mountains. The enemy which was encamped on top of the mountains had a clear view of any movement on the deserts below. From their extremely strong and fortified positions, they kept up an incessant barrage of artillery fire, and machine guns fired their volleys of bullets on us. It was, however, not enough to stop our soldiers. One unit of Australian cavalry managed to advance up the mountains and push back the enemy from their positions. In their wake, foot soldiers with their heavy luggage and guns also made progress fighting smaller battles along the way. It was as if we were relentlessly advancing like water flowing down a mountainside–nothing could stop us. Walking on the desert sands had been a struggle; we were now on the Hebrot mountains, and this was equally challenging. Jumping up and down scrags and hillocks, we were trying to attack enemy positions. If we were on a hill, the enemy would be encamped on the opposite peak and we would slowly try to advance to their positions.

Trekking Ten Miles for Water

Besides fighting, soldiers had to face many other major problems in this battlefield. There was an acute shortage of water. We were practically covered with sand most of the time, and the heat was severe; soldiers were practically dying for water under such circumstances. Since we could not wash ourselves for days on end, our bodies would break out in boils, especially on our forehead. The hair falling on our forehead, covered with sand and sweat, would stick to our skin and cause a lot of pain and abscesses. The situation was so intolerable that we had to take emergency action by shaving the hair off the front of our heads immediately. In fact, special military orders were issued to make sure this happened. When I first received orders that my head was to be shaved,

I stayed inside my tent the whole day, mourning the loss of my beautiful hair. Once in every eight or fifteen days, orders would be issued that, instead of a parade, we were to go and wash our faces. We would be thrilled beyond measure when we heard this. Every day, a small group of soldiers would be issued this order and the regimental band would accompany them during this washing expedition. Singing with the band, we would march for about five miles with our towels and any clothes which had to be washed. Two gallons of water would be given to four soldiers in a waterproof packet. As we did not have any basin, we would dig a hole in the ground where we would pour this water. After having washed our hands and faces, we would wash our underwear and socks in the same dirty water and set them to dry out. Once they dried, we would wear them again and march back to our camp by night. Since the march back would be dusty, by the time we reached camp we would be in the same state as we were when we first set out in the morning. This was the situation we faced for something as essential as water. But as we advanced further into the Hebrot mountains, we were greatly impressed by the arrangements the enemy had made for water.

Secret Wells in the Hebrot Mountains

In these mountainous regions, soldiers had to struggle very hard and march for long distances to get access to water. Sometimes we would get information about a well on a particular hillock, and a patrol would be sent to investigate it. Our group was also frequently sent on such water-searching expeditions. We would walk in a single file, turning over and looking behind every stone very carefully to find any traces of water. Often we would not be able to locate the well and turn back in disappointment. And if we did find water, it would be polluted and not fit for consumption.

We were occupied in this search for many days, and finally we were successful in discovering a fantastic source of water. At first glance, the well seemed completely dry, but we investigated further by sending down lights and throwing stones to hear if there was a splash; not much was achieved by these methods. But one of those stones rolled off further inside and we felt there was a depression. This led us to a more intensive search and we sent a man down into the well. He discovered an underground path which led deeper into the well. This discovery was enough to fire up the soldiers, and many more Tommies jumped in to help him. And what do you think we found? With the joint effort of all these soldiers, we were able to make a great discovery. What had seemed like a dry and empty well had a small passageway which led to an inner cavern that was completely dark but contained a large supply of pure and sparkling water. Can you imagine our delight? This news was conveyed immediately to our base camp and a doctor arrived to examine the water. Only after he had confirmed that it was perfectly safe were we ordered to use the water. After the discovery of this first well, we were able to discover many more such wells that were hidden from gaze. We were amazed by the ingenuity and skill of the enemy in digging them. Besides these wells, there was yet another method to store water in this harsh environment. If the army was to be based in one particular location for a long time, a large cavity, about the size of a small pond, would be dug in front of the camp. It would be lined with thick cloth and filled with water. Soldiers would be provided their ration of water from this pond on a daily basis. This water was brought from great distances on the backs of camels; huge caravans would be employed for this purpose. Each camel would be loaded with two fantas, that is, drums made from sheets of tin, on either side of its hump. Long chains of these animals would come swaying slowly through the desert. The water would be emptied into this pond and stored there. Soldiers were sometimes supplied with their rations early in the morning and sometimes at night. Each soldier was given a bottle of drinking water containing two pints daily; he was free to drink it or to use it in any other manner he thought fit. Sometimes even this limited ration was not available. And our camp abounded in water thieves who were quick to act at the first opportunity. If by chance one didn't hide one's bottle and went off to work elsewhere, one might as well forget about the water. These scoundrels would steal the water-filled bottle and replace it with an empty one. Water thieves were more common in the camp than those who stole money. Whether we got a lesser or greater supply of water depended completely on the camels. If one of these camels died en route, or if it slipped down the mountainside because of heavy rains, and this happened quite frequently, we would have to make do with less water. It was not just water that was in short supply, but the situation was also about the same for food. And once we started camping in the high mountains, we felt that things got worse. At first sight, everything had seemed like fun—the sight of those caravans of camels and those long lines of mules, laden with food, making their steady way up the hills was indeed a diversion in our boring lives.

Lack of Defensive Fortifications—Hiding like Rats

It must have been obvious from the foregoing that we were living in miserable conditions on those mountains. All the fighting took place on the mountains, but it was futile to dig trenches there. We had to build some kind of a defensive position, which was known as a sanga. These sangas were extremely useful during times of battle. It is worth understanding how they were built. During the night, we would gather small stones and large boulders from the surrounding areas and erect a wall about four feet high at a strategic position on the slope. This wall would be built on three sides. Once it was erected, it would be camouflaged by piling dirt and branches and twigs on and around it. If we did not camouflage it, it would have been curtains for us the next morning because the enemy could have easily spotted it and bombarded it to smithereens, and we would have been chickenfeed in the process. In spite of this danger, these little walls were extremely useful. Before the soldiers were sent forward to fight, they were given special instructions on self-protection. If we happened to drive away the enemy from their position on a hill, we were to immediately gather three or four large boulders and arrange them in such a way that they formed a line of first defence. In emergencies, we could hide behind these stones. We once faced this kind of a situation when we had advanced beyond Jerusalem. I might as well describe it here. There was a hill named White Ridge where we had to fight a fierce battle all through the day, but we eventually managed to achieve a bloody triumph by capturing enemy positions on that hill. Our problems started only after we had won. We were about twenty-odd Tommies and were rummaging around in the enemy positions to check if they had left anything behind. During times of battle, it was normal to leave everything as one fled from the enemy. Soldiers who had been seriously wounded would also have to be left behind. On this occasion too, the enemy had fled, leaving behind many injured soldiers. We had bound them together and were about to march them off to our camp as prisoners of war. It was quite likely we could get additional information about the enemy through them. Besides the injured soldiers, there were innumerable other soldiers who had died fighting. We had to leave them where they were. Just as we were occupied in our search-and-rummage operations, the enemy reorganized and suddenly launched a counter-attack on us by firing a shower of bullets. Two of our soldiers immediately fell down injured. One of them was so grievously hurt that he could not move. Unfortunately, we had not taken any of the prescribed precautions for self-protection, and this attack caught us by surprise and we started running helter-skelter. We were desperately searching for a place to hide, perhaps crouch behind a large boulder. We started fighting among ourselves over boulders. We had never imagined that the enemy would regroup and attack us again. We were surrounded by machine-gun fire from three sides, and in a short while, we suffered a lot of casualties. We were now reduced to dire straits; as a final defence, we lay down flat on the ground and positioned boulders in front of our heads. This was perhaps the only way to save ourselves, and we begged God to help us. Each passing minute seemed to bring us closer to death and our hearts were terrorized. Many bullets whizzed past us at hair's breadth distance and some of them hit the stones we had placed in front of ourselves. If they had been placed a few inches this way or that, it would have been goodbye! Did we have any hope of saving ourselves? Each minute was valuable to us; if we hung around there for much longer, it would have meant certain death. Enemy reinforcements would soon arrive to support them, while our main unit which was behind us would not have been in any position to help. As we were caught in the firing space between our positions and the enemy's, the soldiers from the main unit would not have been able to open fire without endangering us. We were caught in an impossible situation, and there was only one solution—to make a dash for our own lines. Once we had decided on this option, we got up one by one to make a dash for it. The first two soldiers who got up ran straight up the mountain instead of running across it. The climb tired them very fast, and they could not make quick enough progress and were soon brought down by enemy bullets. One of them got up again and tried to run but was immediately hit in the hand by two bullets. In spite of this, he was lucky enough to escape with his life. When we saw what had happened to them, our condition became worse, but there was really no other option. Thinking it would be better to die rather than fall into the hands of the enemy, the rest of us also started running. Many of us were shot down but managed to get back on our feet, shouting and screaming. Our pathetic condition would have been enough to move the most stone-hearted of men. Out of the twenty of us, only eight were lucky enough to get back alive without any injuries. After our terrible experience, no soldier dared to make any advance without adequate preparations.

Joint Attack of the Queen's and Middlesex Regiments on White Ridge

The sun had set and it was already dark. On that terrifying night, we suddenly received orders that the A Company and D Company had to get ready for fighting orders. A fighting order meant that we had to don our complete equipment, that is, our cummerbund with its two straps crossed over the shoulders. On the right-hand strap, a full bottle of water was attached. On our backs, we had to tie our haversacks that contained food rations for twenty-four hours. The chest pocket was full of cartridges. Besides, we had to carry two bandoliers that contained an additional one hundred and twenty cartridges each. We also had to pack in a few Mills bombs that might be handy during close combat. Our bayonet had to be hung from the left strap; hanging alongside it would be a wooden 'trenches tool handle' or a small shovel or spade as they can be extremely useful to have at hand during combat. If we had to camp somewhere which was not clean, this tool was very useful for uprooting shrubs and thorny plants from the area. During times of intense hand-to-hand combat, this tool also proved very handy to smash the enemy's forehead, if the situation demanded it! As per the fighting order we had received, the soldiers had to be ready to march at three o'clock in the morning. We were also instructed to have our morning tea and food, as there was no telling when we would get to eat our next meal. The attack was to commence at five o'clock. As the place from where we were to launch our attack was far from our campsite, we had to march quite a distance to get there. The actual attack was to be led by the Queen's Regiment, while we were the reserve force. We were to help them if required. We marched slowly towards the position held by the Queen's, contemplating the possibilities that the day held for us. The Queen's were preparing to move forward when we reached them. We were immediately ordered to load our guns and be in readiness. Just as the orders were being issued to unload the Lewis guns from the backs of the mules and get them battle-ready, our artillery started firing from the lines behind us. Each shell would explode so loudly that we felt our eardrums would be shattered. Soon enough, the enemy returned artillery fire. All of us froze where we stood. But this was only for a very short while, as we heard that orders had been issued to the Queen's to advance and attack. This provoked a great volley of machine-gun fire from the enemy. The sky resounded with the sound of 'Bang! Bang!' and bullets began to whizz past us. In a short while, many injured soldiers from the Queen's Regiment began to hobble back into our lines. The enemy had held on to its position and mounted a resolute defence and wreaked havoc among the soldiers of the Queen's. As many more of them fell to enemy bullets, the Middlesex D Company was ordered to advance to their aid. They moved forward under the cover of heavy bombardment, but the enemy was very strong and held on to its position. Even though there was a tremendous loss of life in the enemy lines, we had also lost a lot of men. There was panic in our lines. Just then we saw our commanding officer walking towards us, twirling his baton, and all our fright vanished and a strange enthusiasm seemed to fill us. When a very senior officer joins the ranks in times of severe distress, it is hardly surprising their confidence receives a great boost. When he saw the straits we were in, he resolved to take the attack right up to the enemy lines. After a consultation between the colonels of the Middlesex and Queen's regiments, the A Company of which I was a part was also ordered to advance. We clicked our bayonets into position and moved forward, only to walk into a very fierce battle on the stony hills. As news filtered through to the soldiers that the commanding officer was present on the front line, it was as if they were recharged to launch the assault with renewed vigour. In this final assault, we were fortunate to be able to dislodge the enemy from its position, but with a great loss of men. However, as we have already seen, the enemy was able to reorganize itself and launch a counter-attack. The enemy mounted eight attacks on us until evening. We were in danger every minute of the day. It seemed like the enemy would dislodge us from our hard-won positions as there were few soldiers from both the regiments who were still able to fight. We were desperately waiting for reinforcements to arrive. Finally, at eight in the night our reliefs arrived and took over our positions.

Bitter Experience in the Fighting Patrol

It was not as if we could rest in peace after this terrifying battle. We finally limped into our camp at about eleven in the night. Another company was getting ready for an assault and were standing in fighting order. These men were going to reconnoitre enemy positions and movements, but this was no ordinary patrol. It was a fighting patrol; in case they were challenged by the enemy, they had to be in a position to fight back and were, therefore, fully equipped. This group of about twenty-five to thirty men under the command of an officer would venture out of our lines and spread out along the line of control and patrol the area. In like manner, the enemy also sent its fighting patrol, and on occasion, these two patrols would encounter each other. They might end up engaging each other and a gruesome hand-to-hand battle would take place. But if the enemy numbers were more than ours, we would have to hide behind some large stones and let them pass unchallenged. We could feel our hearts beating heavily as they passed us by. In some lines, the patrolling would have to be done all through the night. As one party returned, the next group would set off. When these patrols set out, our sentries had to be informed that a patrol from such and such company will set out at a particular hour and return at a designated hour. When a patrol returned, the sentries were immediately informed of their arrival. This was to avoid situations where our own men were fired at by sentries when they sensed any movement beyond our lines. Besides these fighting patrols, in some lines search patrols had to be sent. The soldiers in the search patrols were particularly brave and courageous. About two to four soldiers would form a search patrol. I remember one particular occasion when three of us stepped out under the command of an officer to obtain information on enemy positions. Their positions were on the hills, about a mile away from our line. Early in the morning, we could see them patrolling the hills. We had, however, received secret information that they did not actually hold any positions on those hills. The objective of our patrol was to confirm this news. Once the orders were issued, our friends subjected us to a lot of questions. Some of them were proud of us while others called us mad to have volunteered for such a task. At any rate, when we were getting ready to leave, everybody made it a point to be very solicitous as there was a high probability that we might not return the next morning. Before stepping out, a bottle of rum was served to us to help us remain alert. At two o'clock in the dead of the night, we slowly started on our assignment. It was pitch dark that night and a light breeze swayed the shrubs on the hills; it felt like they were enemy soldiers ready to give us the final charge. None of us were afraid of death, but we would rather not be captured by the enemy. It was highly likely that the enemy was hiding behind any of the numerous boulders strewn around the place. How were we to know where they were? Each step had to be taken very carefully and silently as we could be surrounded by the enemy at any time during the patrol. As our fortunes were on the ascendancy, we were able to reach the peak where we had suspected the enemy was based. At that point, it started raining lightly. This was to our benefit as our steps would be muffled by the rain. It was also just possible that the sentries on duty at the enemy posts might have taken shelter from the rain and were not keeping guard. Even though we were soaked to the skin, we marched on ahead, hoping to capitalize on any advantage the rain might offer us. We now moved forward in a diamond formation–one soldier would lead the way, while the other three would be about ten yards behind him, one directly behind while the other two were a few steps away to the right and the left. In this way, we could monitor all four directions. If the leading soldier stopped in his tracks, the others would also stop where they were. Each step was taken very calculatedly only after we had monitored all four directions. Every so often, our fingers would play on the trigger. Ah! Now what? The first soldier was lying flat on his stomach; we froze where we stood and then lay down on the ground, which was covered with rainwater, and advanced forward to reach our companion. As we joined him, it felt as if our blood had frozen in our veins; we could hear voices just a little ahead of us! Hmm! If we had taken a few more steps, we would have walked straight into the enemy's line of fire. Because of the rain, they had taken shelter under a tree.

If they had had any inkling of our presence, I certainly would not have been around to write this book. Since we were caught in a very delicate situation, we withdrew as quietly as we could and slid down the hillside. We were so shaken by this experience that we could hardly find our footing on the way back. Slipping over stones and rocks, we could not afford to make any noise as we scrambled back. On the one hand, we were worried about tripping and having a bad fall, and on the other, we were worried about the volley of bullets that could hit our backs at any moment. If, God forbid, one of us should break a leg, what was to be done? Who would have been able to carry him back? Only after we got down the hillside and crossed the dark valley did we get our voices back and realized we were soaking wet from the rain and bleeding from injuries sustained during our scramble. Until then, we had lost all sense of what was happening to us.

14

The Conquest of Jerusalem

Let us turn our attention to the Turkish soldiers. The Turks of Turkestan seem to be very different from the Muslims settled in Hindustan. With their handsome faces and their smart uniforms and their stiff Turkish caps, there is no doubt that the Turkish soldiers present a very impressive appearance.

The Bravery of Turkish Soldiers

When it comes to fighting, the Turks are hardly pushovers. They seem to be capable of very brave acts when the occasion demands. Let me relate an incident from our White Ridge campaign which will illustrate their behaviour on the battlefield. When we mounted our assault on the White Ridge, the Turks put up a very stiff defence. Even after we had reached the very top of the ridge, five Turkish soldiers held their positions and continued to shower bullets on us and tried their very best to prevent our advance. One of them did not even have a rifle, but it did not stop him from attacking us. He picked up a huge boulder and aimed it at us. Unluckily, at that moment, his companions gave up the fight and ran away. He, however, continued to hold his position but he was finally overcome and had to surrender. When we had the chance to encounter a professional soldier from the original Turkish Army, he seemed brave and able. Sadly, there were very few of them left. During the early battles of this war, they had suffered heavy losses. By 1917, the Turkish Army was mainly made up of new recruits who seemed very unorganized and in an unprepared state. Many of them did not have proper clothing; only a few of them had boots, while many of the poor soldiers were wasting away without boots.

A Cannon Assembled in Three Minutes

Let us review the weapons that were used in this bloody war to wreak havoc on humans. This mountain war was of a very different character, and its weaponry was also specific to the conditions. The most important of these weapons was the mounted battery–artillery guns mounted on mules. They really came into their own in these battles and terrorized the enemy ranks. There were many areas on this scraggy hillside where the large mortar guns just could not be hauled, and in times of danger, they could not be withdrawn as quickly as one desired. A different strategy had to be adopted for this terrain. Guns which could be completely knocked down were employed in this theatre of war. Each of the components of the gun–the barrel, the iron support for the barrels, and other parts–would be separately loaded on to the backs of mules and transported to the top of the mountains. This gun could then be assembled in three minutes and would be ready to start firing. It had the capabilities of a 6-incher and wrought much the same destruction on the enemy. Its shells were similar to those of 6-inch howitzers, and as it could be used right on the front lines, it proved to be a lot more dangerous and caused a lot of bloodshed. The enemy was equally prompt in returning mortar fire, and the poor soldiers on the front lines from both sides had to bear the brunt of the deadly mounted battery. These fantastic shells had a larger impact on those mountains as they would explode on the huge boulders which would shatter into a thousand pieces, each one of them deadlier than a bullet. In front of such firepower, an ordinary soldier was helpless.

Artillery Guns on the Battlefields

Besides these mounted batteries, we also had to rely on the regular artillery guns during this war. It was extremely difficult to transport these huge guns into the actual arena of fighting. The soldiers had to exert themselves to overcome this difficulty. The movement of guns and shells (which were loaded on mules) required proper roads. How were these large guns to be transported in the absence of roads? The terrain was all sharp slopes and high peaks. The thankless task of flattening a road for these guns also fell to the unfortunate soldiers. Two companies would be assigned the morning shift while the other two companies would be assigned the night shift. This would mean hoisting our spades and shovels on our shoulders and walking for two to four miles to get to the site. We would have to make a level path and fill up any depressions that might obstruct the progress of the guns. Let me have you know that it was hardly a walk in the park. Lifting and moving huge boulders, gathering smaller stones to fill up the depressions, and then levelling them out was a killing job. As soon as we managed to construct a rough road of sorts, mules with shells laden on their backs would be driven over it and the heavy guns would trundle on behind them. Baskets made of reeds were tied to both sides of the mules, and each of them would carry four or six shells. It was not as if there were one or two mules; they would number in the thousands. During times of emergency, an entire brigade would be pressed into building roads. No need for a Shepherd Miners or a Pioneer Company! The foot soldiers were made to do all the grinding work. On most days, we would spend the entire day from sunrise to sunset on the job. If it happened to rain, things would get miserable; but this did not mean we stopped work. Though soaked to the skin, we would just get on with it. In the evening, when we trekked back the same distance to our camps, further misery was eagerly awaiting our return. The relentless rain would have uprooted our small tents and the wind would be blowing them hither-thither. If there was no tent to cover them, can you imagine the condition of our belongings? Would they be dry? After having worked hard all through the day, it was very painful that we now had to struggle to erect our tents on wet ground wearing wet clothes. But if everything was soaking wet, how were we to relax? The clothes on our body were wet, the ground was wet, our blankets were wet. Is it surprising that this situation drove the poor soldiers crazy, and they would curse this terrible war?

Malarial Fever

Since we had to spend entire days in this miserable cold and poisonous air, could disease be far behind? Malarial fever was very common among the soldiers in this theatre of war and they suffered a lot. Many soldiers would collapse even as they were marching due to it. They would start shivering with cold and run a high fever. The situation would suddenly take a turn for the worse and the soldiers would fall like ninepins. The number of soldiers who were infected by malaria became so high that many hospitals were designated as exclusive malaria hospitals. But as these hospitals also began to overflow with patients, the soldiers would be sent back to their regiments within a very short while. As ill luck would have it, this fever would never be completely cured and the poor soldiers continued to suffer. But was there anybody to hear their complaints?

Long-Tail Bombs

Bombs played a major part in this mountain warfare. In this terrifying war, many kinds of bombs were invented, but it was not as if all of them could be used in every theatre of war. The British Army's Mills bomb was very effective in the battlefields of France, but those grenades had to be lobbed by hand and were not particularly useful in this theatre. While grenades lobbed by hand would land about forty to fifty yards away, a range of four to five hundred yards was necessary in these mountains. So these bombs, the latest invention of the white brain, were converted so that they could be used as rifle grenades.

Barbed Wire

As our brains are now obsessed with bombs, we might as well consider how these weapons of destruction were put to other uses in this war. Your brain had to be twisted in a special way to think of such uses. This was a battle whose main objective was the destruction of life, and these new innovations were based on this very principle. One of the most effective strategies was the use of barbed wire. Soldiers would be ordered to carry out this assignment at night. Hiding in the dark of the night, our group would hoist huge bundles of barbed wire and set about laying a wall of it. These walls would be erected on the lower slopes of the hills where we were camped. This was a very challenging and dangerous task. Besides laying out the barbed wire, we would insert small bombs at intervals on the ground near it. They would be placed in such a way that if somebody stepped on them or some other pressure was applied, they would explode. In case the enemy approached our lines and tried to cut and clear the barbed wire, the bombs would explode due to their movements, thus injuring them and warning us of an imminent attack. This forewarning would be sufficient for us to prepare our defences. However, there was a likelihood that this strategy could backfire. When our patrols stepped out for their nightly reconnaissance, they would have to pass through this barbed-wire fencing. It was fairly easy to miss a step in the night and set off a bomb.

Launching an Attack on the Mountains

Life and death was a matter of chance in this war, and when we leapt from one peak to another trying to push back the enemy, life had indeed become very cheap. The state of the common soldiers when we had to advance our positions had to be seen to be believed. I might as well narrate a specific incident that will provide an idea about this experience. On a particular morning, our C Company received orders to attack a hill in the neighbourhood of Tel-a-zu, a mountain in Palestine. To get to this hill, an open and flat ground of about a thousand yards had to be traversed before one could start climbing up. Perhaps the stars were aligned against us, but it was very dusty from the early morning, and a thick fog descended into the valley. But orders had been issued and there was no turning back. Visibility was so low that we could barely see our own hands. All the lower reaches were heavy with fog, and as the soldiers bravely ventured forward, they were disoriented by it. On the one hand, they had to be sure of their footing as they tried to reach their target, while on the other, they had to face the volley of bullets let loose by the machine guns of the enemy. They also had to contend with artillery fire. What were the poor sods to do but die? From their position on top of the peak, the enemy observed the performance of our soldiers as if they had got the best seats for the matinee show. When our poor soldiers tried to ascend the peak, they would pick them off one by one with their bullets. The only other option for our soldiers was to lie down where they were, but they could not escape death even then as the enemy would start using their machine guns. Many soldiers would come hurtling down the slopes after they were hit by machine-gun fire, while others would give up the ghost right where they were. A single machine gun could release five hundred bullets per minute, and if such a large number of guns were firing simultaneously, what was an ordinary human being to do? And as this was an everyday occurrence, would anybody take any particular notice of it? In this great war, machine guns wreaked havoc and caused a lot of misery to the soldiers. If in the flash of a second, five hundred bullets come 'Bang! Bang!' at you, can you imagine your condition? One or two of these guns were enough to stop an entire platoon in its tracks. The management of these guns was organized in such a way that the firing was incessant. Three men were assigned to each gun—the first one to fire it, the second as a backup in case the first one died or was injured, the third ready at hand to reload it once the ammunition belt was exhausted. This would take hardly two or three seconds, and the gun would be ready to get back into action. In front of these monstrous guns, the soldiers were like sitting ducks.

'Fall In, Teek Party'

This phrase was a very common one in the army. If anything happened, a 'teek' was formed. If some men were required in the officers' mess, a teek party would be formed. It was as if a gang of labourers were being pressed to work. You had a separate teek party to clean the knives and forks in the officers' mess, another one to scrub the pots and pans in the sergeants' mess, and another one to wash the tables and chairs in the canteen. And if we had to move camp and luggage had to be loaded on camels, it was yet another teek party. The toon sergeant would call out your name in a loud booming voice and you had to fall in. It often happened that you had just walked into camp after marching for ten to fifteen miles and had not yet got the kit off your back, when you would hear your name being called out loudly and you would realize it meant 'fall in, teek party'. Firstly, there would be a teek party to unload rifles from a camel caravan, and just as it would get done, orders would be issued for tents to be sent up for our own stay; and just as we were catching our breath, the orderly corporal would shout for us to 'fall in, mess orderly', and we had no option but to run. But there were worse things in store for us. Just imagine, you hobble back into camp after taking part in a major battle and having cheated death by a whisker many times over–you could be sure that teek orders would be issued late in the night. We very well knew what this was about–it meant we had to return to the scene of the bloody battle and haul back the cold corpses of the brave soldiers who had sacrificed their lives. Not only was this a very arduous task, it also gave us the creeps.

The corpses would have to be carried from distant places in the surrounding mountains. As we hauled the bodies back, it sent shivers down our spine. The soldiers also had to dig the graves for these corpses. If a soldier lost his life during battle, his body would be buried in the same condition it had been found in–with his army uniform, boots and other paraphernalia. This was considered a particular honour. But if an injured soldier was to die after he had been shifted from the scene of battle, he could not claim this honour. He was buried in the normal manner. If a soldier were to die in a military hospital, then he would be accorded a military funeral in line with his rank. This was a very impressive performance–the coffin containing the body would be placed on a caisson and draped with the Union Jack. A military band would lead the procession while playing the death march. Soldiers would march ahead of the vehicle in two columns with arms reversed as a sign of mourning. Once the body reached the grave, a final salute would be offered before the guns were lowered. Finally, the sombre tunes of the 'Last Post' would be played on the bugle, producing a very grave effect on the audience. If one has to die, let it be like this.

A Resounding Welcome to the British Army in the Historic City of Zion

After many years of hard fighting, the victorious army of our king finally took control of the lands of Palestine and Egypt and entered the historic city of Jerusalem. Was there anybody who was not delighted by this turn of events? There were many soldiers in our regiment who were unluckier than I was. They had spent over two years in this theatre of war–all they had seen was the sand and the sky. You can well imagine their joy, after years in the wilderness, at getting back to civilization, especially one of the oldest cities known to man. It would be easier to imagine rather than describe their feelings. Everybody felt they had entered heaven after a long spell in hell. One could also sense a wave of enthusiasm sweeping through the citizens of Jerusalem. When our army was led into the city by our military band on a fine morning, the citizens clambered to the rooftops to get a proper look at us. What does the British Army look like? The soldiers were equally delighted. The valleys beside the roads were covered with vines heavy with grapes and fig trees laden with fruit. The beautiful buildings on the hillsides presented a fair sight. The tinkling of bells as farmers led their horses out to the farms was music to our ears. While all the

Tommies were excited by this new experience, my heart leapt with joy. It was this very city which had been conquered by the ancient Persian emperors, and I was following in their footsteps. Here I was, a Zoroastrian soldier with a gun hoisted on my shoulder, entering the city over which flew the flag of the great British sovereign; who would not be proud to be here? This was the holy land that was conquered by the famous Persian emperor, Khusro Pervez, in 614, who opened, as it were, an account for the Parsis in this city. This clearly demonstrates that we Parsis also have a stake in this city. There was a time when the Persian standard fluttered over the ramparts of this city proclaiming our victory.

15
A Tourist in Jerusalem

Over the centuries, Jerusalem has been known by many different names. The Jews call it Yarushalom, while in Pahlavi texts the city is known as Ochiselam. The Greek books call it Hierosolyma. Just as different writers have used a variety of names for it, the city has also passed through many ups and downs. Although it has been reduced to rubble repeatedly, it has still managed to survive. In spite of Lady Luck having put her through the grind, Jerusalem continues to be famous throughout the world.

Old Jerusalem

This ancient city is built on four hills. Mount Zion was settled during the time of the Jebusites. Mount Moriha is a little towards the east of Mount Zion and a little lower than it. There are many beautiful mosques on this hill presently. Towards the north-east of the city is Mount Bezetha, which is higher than Mount Moriha. Mount Acro is in the north-western part of the city. This gives the city a rectangular shape and adds to its beauty. The views in every direction are spectacular. And if you look downwards, you can see frighteningly steep valleys covered with greenery.

The Turkish Railways

Jerusalem is not a very big city. Let us leave the war behind for just a little while and take this opportunity to tour this city and have a little fun and see the ancient sites in Jerusalem. Before the war, there was nothing like a railway network in Palestine, just a couple of railway lines. The Jerusalem–Ramla line, which had a narrow gauge, had managed to reach Gaza. During the war, the enemy uprooted and destroyed this line as it retreated. But it was the war which changed the fortunes of the railways. It is now possible to travel by rail on an excellent train running from Alexandria to Jerusalem. No more of those tiresome camel safaris on the sandy deserts. And no more having to camp overnight at those staging points in great discomfort. If nothing else, the Great War has proved to be a great boon to this city. You might ask: Does this distant city have any need for a railway station? You would, however, be shocked at the sight of the impressive Jerusalem station. As you step out of the station, you see the main road that leads to the city. It would take you about an hour to reach the city, but if you would rather ride, you could get into a carriage hauled by two mules. But why would a soldier like me need a vehicle? I just kept walking along the road that goes uphill. This road leads to the old city, while another road which branches out to the left takes you to the newer parts. Let us take a look at the old city first. Once you reach the top, the first building on the left is a Mohammedan hotel or inn. The fun-loving locals are playing a game of chess right on the road and are being rather boisterous. As you walk on, you will notice a variety of shops that are managed by Jews.

My First Experience with a Jewish Woman

I might as well tell you that it is extremely risky to stand outside a shop managed by a Jewish woman. If you happen to be outside one of these shops, a young comely Jewish woman will soon emerge from the shop, make eyes at you and talk to you so sweetly that you will have no alternative but to follow her in. And once you step inside, she won't let you leave unless you buy something. You should take this for a fact since this was my personal experience. And since I could not make a swift escape, I decided to purchase a few picture postcards. And without thinking, I offered her a pound note with a flourish. But would she let me off so easily? She immediately took the note, and in her tinkling voice, told me I should buy some more stuff as she did not have any change. She suggested rather coolly that I should buy a pound's worth of goods. I tried very hard to squirm my way out of this situation but she wouldn't let me escape. I ended up buying a pound's worth of postcards. I left that unlucky guinea there and returned having learnt a new lesson. Those postcards are still rotting in my house. There does not seem to be any practice of giving any change back if you offer a guinea note in this city. These Jewish women can be rather ruthless in such matters. Even though this is a rather remote location with hardly any traffic from the centres of fashion, they seem to be quite fashionable here. You can see the locals strolling in the evening, dressed to the nines. However, these rather well-built Jewish women did not particularly appeal to my tastes. I wonder why their faces are so pale in colour. And anyway, why should women be so muscular?

How Jews Earn Money in Hotels and Restaurants

Having experienced their shops, one might as well pop into a Jewish restaurant. Before the advent of the British Army, the city was rather listless with hardly any economic activity. But with the coming of the British, the fortunes of the Jews have changed for the better. An area in which the Jews have taken the lead is in small hotels and restaurants. In Mumbai, we can enjoy a cup of tea for one paisa, but here it will cost you two piastres, or about five annas. One piastre is about two and a half annas. It will get you a biscuit or a little cake. I could gobble a hundred such cakes and it would make no difference to my appetite. If you go to an ordinary restaurant and have a light dinner, it will set you back by fifteen piastres or two and a half rupees. Even a posh hotel in London would not be so expensive! But if you are looking for something cheap in this country, you could try oranges, grapes, melons and figs. They grow in such profusion that there is no way all of them can be consumed.

The Old Fort and Its Seven Gates

There is nothing much to see in the newer parts of the city. But when we enter the old city, we find it is practically a museum of ancient buildings. The first thing that catches your attention is the fort encircling the old city. It reminded me of the Great Wall of China. You might ask: What is there to see in a wall? But at least you can walk on top of it. The wall of this fort is about thirty-five feet high and about three to four feet wide at places. Two people can walk abreast on top of it. There are thirty-four watchtowers on the wall. These pagoda-like structures are excellent examples of the original construction. There are eight gates through which one can enter the city. Each gate has a unique name which identifies its purpose. The first gate through which one can enter the city is the Jaffa Gate. It is big enough for an elephant to pass under it. The second gate was built by the German emperor Kaiser Wilhelm twenty-five years ago. A third gate has been opened near it recently by Field Marshal Earl Allenby to commemorate the conquest of Jerusalem. The road leading from the Jaffa Gate connects Jerusalem to the city of Jaffa.

The Historic Golden Gate

Besides the Jaffa Gate, there are six other gates in the old fort. They have been given different names. The last of these is the Golden Gate or the Close Gate. The gate is believed to have existed from the time of King Justinian. There are strong iron grilles on either side of this gate. It is said that the prophet Christ passed through this gate on a Sunday. It had been the practice for many years for pilgrims going to the temple to enter through this gate on Sundays. They can, however, exit from whichever gate they prefer. When entering through this gate, one had to climb two hundred steep steps, and it used to take nearly an hour to ascend them. There would always be a crowd of people here and they would sing songs as they climbed slowly. But after the Sultan of Turkey closed this gate, it has not yet been opened for anyone. The roads in the old city are a maze. If you happen to go in without a guide, you could wander the whole day without being able to find an exit. As the roads are paved with the original stone which has been totally worn down, you have to be very careful while walking, or else you could find your nose rubbing against the stones.

The Swinging Wooden Bridge under the Ground

And what's this new thing? Be careful! There is no shortage of ancient historical monuments in this city. Out of these, the

Tower of Siloam is quite amazing. You can see the sky above you and the water below. Even a stout-hearted man would tremble to enter this place. After walking past a small Greek temple, we encounter a door on our left, which is always closed. One need not turn back disappointed, because one can enter through a small gate next to it. As we go ahead, we see a tower which is completely in ruins. It is said that when the tower collapsed, eighteen people were crushed underneath it. Only God knows the truth. However, one can see a tunnel below that can be accessed by a flight of stairs of sixteen steps. After climbing down these steps, one can see a decrepit wooden bridge which is about fifty-three feet long and eighteen feet wide. If one looks towards the left, one realizes the bridge has been built between two walls. As the water is another nineteen feet below, one might wonder why this bridge has been built. I could never figure out why. But let's go further to the right. One climbs down thirteen steps to go deeper into the tunnel. It is so cold here that one begins to wonder what kind of cold hell is this. The stairs are so worn out that it is scary to step on them. Water comes up to the last step and it seems a pond has been built between two walls. We can now see the wooden bridge, which presents a rather scary sight. The walls are also very cold. If we touch them, our heart feels cold and we start shivering. The real story behind the bridge is that many years ago a blind man had come here. He had a vision that if he washed his face with the water, he would regain his eyesight. The man went up to the lake and washed his face, and promptly regained his sight. God knows if it is true! How much fun would it be if this miracle worked even now? Our poor dear eye doctors would be rendered jobless. But how would we let go of the fashion of wearing eyeglasses?

The Dead Sea

You might wonder how a sea could die. But, my dear friend, the world is full of the strangest curiosities. How can you see them unless you step out of your village? One of the highlights of Palestine is the sea of salt. The Dead Sea is visible at a distance from the Bethlehem Road, which branches off the main road just before entering Jerusalem. This sea is 1,300 feet lower than the Mediterranean Sea. And what about the water in this strange sea? It is considered to be the heaviest water in the world. This sea is said to be forty-six English miles in length and about nine and a half miles wide. The water in this sea seems to be the dirtiest in the world. It's so heavy that you cannot move freely in it. The water in the interior is so salty and bitter that if you happened to ingest just a little bit of it, you would spend the rest of the day vomiting. According to experts in chemical sciences, it is seventy parts water and thirty parts salt. If you drink this water every day, you will have no need for a purgative. Neither can shipping vessels ply in its waters, nor can anyone enter it. Even expert swimmers have been foxed by this sea as its waters are too heavy to swim in. But many pilgrims take vows to wash themselves in it. Even if they cannot actually enter the sea, they do have to make an attempt. But how is one to take a bath? The water is so harsh that when it touches your skin, it breaks into a rash accompanied by a burning sensation. Special arrangements for bathing have been made for pilgrims at the mouth of the river Jordan as the water in its vicinity is not as salty as the rest of the Dead Sea.

Many pilgrims fill bottles with water from the Dead Sea and take them home to sprinkle it in their front yards. The sea also yields a variety of curiosities, including colourful stones. These beautiful stones are cleaned and fashioned into curios, which are exported to other countries.

The Final Resting Place of Christ

If a traveller, who has come all the way to Jerusalem after a lot of huffing and puffing, does not visit the world-famous Holy Church, he would be considered an idiot. This is the final resting place of that world-famous man, Christ. Devotees travel thousands of miles, undergo various kinds of hardship, and spend a lot of money to come to Jerusalem for a glimpse of his tomb. I have personally visited quite a few Christian temples, but it was only in this temple that the atmosphere of sorrow and piety made a deep impression on me. This temple, which is thousands of years old, has seen many ups and downs, undergone many tribulations, and passed through the hands of many kings. It was first built by the great emperor Constantine in the year 335 of the Christian Era. History tells us it was destroyed three times thereafter. When our Iranian emperor Khusro Pervez conquered Jerusalem in the year 614, he also destroyed this temple. He took many of the exquisite antiquities stored in this church with him to Iran. It was rebuilt again in the year 630. Unfortunately, it was again destroyed by fire in the year 967. And the little that survived was ransacked by the Mohammedans in 1010. In spite of all these calamities, it somehow seems to have survived. After a few years, it was rebuilt on a grand scale at great expense by the Crusaders in 1103. But let's not get bogged down by history. Let us just examine the interiors of this temple. Entering the old city through the Jaffa Gate, we turn to the left to get a first look at this world-famous temple. The exteriors of this temple, which has seen twelve hundred Diwalis, are in ruins. The external walls are considered to be part of the original temple and have been retained. After crossing the large courtyard in front of the temple, the first structure we see when we enter it is the tomb of Philip d'Aubigny who died in 1236. He is considered to be an important man in the history of England. The best time to see this church is before ten o'clock in the morning when the crowds begin to arrive. About ten yards ahead, we see a tomb-like structure made of brown marble. It is said that after Christ was brought down from the cross, his body was first placed on this spot. This structure, the Stone of Anointing, was built in the year 1818 to commemorate this incident. We then arrive at the Rotunda, which is considered to be the centre of the church. A huge dome, said to have been built in 1868, has been erected over the Rotunda. This new dome had to be erected as the previous one was destroyed by a fire in 1808. The diameter of the dome is 65 metres. Our attention is drawn to another temple, located adjacent to the dome, which is about 26 feet long and 12 feet wide, and made of marble. It is time to enter this structure with a certain sense of solemnity.

The Sorrow-Inducing Door

Ah! The heart is beating wildly! The atmosphere in this church calls for utmost seriousness. Through a small door, we enter this little church where the great prophet lies peacefully in eternal sleep. Before entering the room where he is buried, one has to pass through three small doors. This tiny temple is known as the Chapel of Angels. A few steps ahead, there is another small door. The only way to pass through this door is to bend forward. On entering the next chamber, we see yet another door which is very tiny, barely four square feet in area. When we first spot it, the question that occurs to us is: Can we pass through it? But since we are keen on going further ahead, we drop to our knees and try to slide and shuffle through it. This is the final door. The innermost chamber is considered to be one of the most holy places in the world. Not only do we feel exalted to arrive here, we are also overcome by a deep sense of sorrow. Ah! What a great place we have entered! There is a high tomb to the left, made of a single piece of marble. Just one stone? It is said that the great prophet Christ is buried under this stone. What an eternal silence! The effect is so melancholic that even the most stone-hearted man would not be able to hold back his tears. No other place has ever made such an impression on me. No ornamentation or pomp! It is a tomb that is most suitable for this great man. No noise or hustle-bustle! The chamber is so tiny that it cannot accommodate even five men at one go. A priest is always present in the chamber. Even the doors which lead up to this chamber are so small that two men cannot pass through them simultaneously. It is as if a blanket of silence has been spread over the chamber. This grave has been built in a very curious manner. Because of its special architecture, howsoever important one may be—even an emperor—one has no option but to bend double before the tomb. Pitiless world! Your ways are indeed strange! Nobody is exempt from your cruel fate, be he an emperor or a prophet!

An Image Worth 30,000 Guineas

Some might say that I am bluffing, while others might say that I am prone to exaggeration! But no, you have to believe me! This temple is full of the most amazing things. After having exited the little chapel, we return to the Rotunda. As we go ahead, we come to another temple known as the Chapel of Syrian. As soon as we enter the temple, we are left astounded. Wow! It is full of the most valuable specimens of workmanship whose wonders I cannot even begin to describe. The beautiful images that are placed in the temple are said to be worth thousands of guineas. In the centre is a sculpture of the prophet Christ in a prone position, which is plated with gold and silver. When you see it for the first time, you stand there agape at the splendour. It is said to have been presented by the Czar of Russia. How much do you think it costs?

A mere thirty thousand guineas! A little less than half a million of our rupees! You could buy the whole of Navsari with this sum of money. But why talk of money? If the glass behind which this image is placed shatters into a thousand pieces, there are enough people who are willing to pay thousands of rupees for each shard. Christians have this kind of blind devotion for every object in this temple. But moving on, there are four other images that are placed in the same case, which are also worth thousands of rupees. Yet another treasure in this hall of curiosities is a candlestick. Yes, a candlestick! It is just a stand on which you place candles, but the devotees seem to have great respect for it and think it to be very unique. It was presented by Queen Helena. It shines so brightly as if its surface has been studded with blue sapphires and diamonds. Carved out of a single stone of agate, it stands eight feet tall. How large do you think the candles for this stand would be? Each of them is about three feet long and so thick that your fingers cannot go around them. If all this had not been explained to me when I entered the room, a country bumpkin like me would never have guessed it was a candlestick. I would have thought it was a pillar encrusted with sapphires and diamonds. You can well imagine the cost of this candlestick yourself. Oh my God! The world is full of treasures. If only I had taken just one of these objects with me, wouldn't my life have been spent in the lap of luxury?

The Prison of Christ

After having seen the house of wonders, I walked down many streets to reach the 'Bone of Christ', which is where Christ was imprisoned. Before Christ was nailed to the cross, he had been hauled into a prison. This place has been maintained in its original state. Thousands of people arrive from great distances to see this spot. This place is inside a cave located on a hillside. Since it is very dark inside, one has to hold a lighted candle before venturing inside. The small cave is in the form of a room where a white stone has been embedded in the floor. A window-like frame has been erected over it in such a manner that a man can stand on the stone if he is bent forward. The white stone has two depressions big enough for human feet to be placed in them. It is said that these are the impressions of the feet of Christ as he stood supporting himself on the frame. Well, only God knows the truth. The people here are fanatically devoted to all the religious objects in this place and are quite willing to sacrifice everything for them.

The Cross on Which Christ Was Crucified

These sights seem to have scared you, dear friends! How are you to roam the world if you are already tired? Now that we have decided to see the historical sites of this place, we might as well see all of them. After exiting the frightening prison, you walk ahead and descend a flight of twenty-nine stairs, which have been completely worn out. If you happen to lose your footing, you will slide all the way down. The interiors are in an equally dilapidated state. They could collapse today, or maybe a couple of days later. But as the old proverb goes, old is gold. The columns are said to date from the times of Emperor Constantine. To see them is to be transported to another era. With fear in our hearts, we step forward gingerly only to come face to face with a cave. The opening of the cave is about ten feet high and around twenty feet wide. I must truthfully confess that I was quite scared to enter the cave. You may or may not believe me, but I am not ashamed to tell the truth. If I stood rooted where I was, I wouldn't be able to see the place. And it would be such a shame to return without seeing it. Frightened as I was, I lit a candle and walked in with a prayer on my lips. Thanks be to Allah that I entered the cave! If Queen Helena could personally inspect this site 1,600 years ago, how could I skip it? It is said that Queen Helena took the lead in the search for the cross on which Christ was crucified. As a result, three crosses were discovered in this cave. Out of these three crosses, one is considered to be the real one. Only God knows the truth behind all this! But whatever be the truth, I was disgusted by the sight of people showering kisses when they saw the cross. Isn't this column rather lucky? But what does history tell us? According to historical accounts, when the Iranian emperor Khusro Pervez conquered Jerusalem in the year 614, he had sent the true cross and other valuable objects to Iran. The true cross was later sent to the Pope at Rome. But there is no definitive source which says that the cross was later returned to Jerusalem from Rome. At any rate, in commemoration of this event, Queen Helena erected a stone monument and a beautiful copper cross at this site. She also placed a statue of herself with an inscription in Latin to perpetuate her memory.

The Statue Studded with Stones Worth Millions

There are numerous things to see in this temple. Returning from the Greek temple, we turn to the right and reach a place known as Calvary. This place is slightly elevated, about fourteen feet higher than the surrounding ground. This is the place where the great prophet Christ was crucified, that is, nailed to a cross. A marble stone has now been placed at this site. It has three holes and it is said that the cross on which Christ was crucified had been erected in the central hole. And the incorrigibly curious traveller is allowed to insert his hand into the hole. Behind this stone, a huge cross has been erected, on which a life-sized statue of the prophet with his hands nailed to the cross has been placed to recreate the crucifixion. This pitiable tableau makes a deep impression on every traveller who gets enveloped by sorrow. Adjacent to Calvary is the

Chapel of Saint Mary, where a huge image of Christ's mother has been placed in a glass case. It seems like she is actually witnessing the death of her son and is mourning his fate. Her sorrowing face draws the attention of every traveller. Many pilgrims have deep faith in the power of this statue and make valuable offerings such as gold bracelets and chains to her. I have personally seen such offerings within the glass case and also hanging from the hands and neck of the statue.

The Famous Mosque of Omar at Jerusalem

On exiting this church, we can see the famous Mosque of Omar about fifty paces ahead. Its workmanship is exquisite. If there is any one object which adds to the beauty of Jerusalem, it is this mosque. It has been known by various names in the past, but it is currently recognized popularly as the Mosque of Omar. When Caliph Omar conquered Jerusalem in the year 637, he erected a small wooden structure at this spot. A little later, its fortunes changed with those of Jerusalem, and in the year 688, Abdul Malik, at great expense, built the structure that is presently standing. There are four doors through which this mosque can be entered. The walls of the building are covered with marble tiles. But the highlight of the workmanship is the six different colours which grab our attention. One does not feel like moving one's gaze from them. Although it has been nearly 1,200 years, it seems like they have been freshly painted. The European travellers, shifting here and there to get the best view, use binoculars to admire these colours from a distance. And then there are others who haul their cameras from one place to another and annoy the bystanders. When one enters the mosque, one can see its impressive dome. The entire structure is supported by twenty-eight columns, sixteen on the outside and twelve on the inside. The dome is ninety-eight feet high. But the most exquisite feature of this building is its glass windows, about thirty-six of them. If you examine the glass carefully, you will notice the beautiful designs and colours that are still intact. And it seems that the colours of the lush Turkish carpets spread on the floor meld with the colours of the windows. These carpets, into which the feet sink up to the knees, have been specially presented by the Sultan of Turkey. Having seen all of this, we advance another fifty steps before we are stopped by a grille made of shining copper rods. This enclosure leads to a small gate, and passing through it, we enter the most holy place in the mosque. The Mohammedans consider the stone inside this room to have miraculous powers. Devotees make a variety of offerings to this brown stone and have worn it down by kissing it. The stone is about sixty feet tall, nearly forty-five feet wide, and proportionally thick. A protective frame of olive wood surrounds it and magnifies its mystery. A cavity has been excavated below this stone and you can see the base of the stone if you enter this cavity. But do not forget to light your candle before entering as it is extremely dark inside. If you slip and fall, you might land in a heap at the bottom. People used to be afraid of venturing below this stone as there was a chance the supporting stones might give way and they would be crushed. There is really nothing to see inside, but you would lose nought by taking a look. The place is considered to be very holy. Towards the right, there is a small room whose walls are lined with stone. There is a small stone platform in the room on which, it is said, the prophets used to sit and offer prayers. Turning back from here, we see an attic-like room at a height, where two ancient copies of the Quran inscribed in iron are said to be deposited.

The Mosque of Al-Aqsa

When we emerge from the Mosque of Omar, we do not have to bother to wear our boots, because we have to visit yet another mosque right opposite it–the Mosque of Al-Aqsa. Be prepared to see a few strange things in this mosque. One has to cross a large courtyard paved with marble and pass by a fountain that sprays water to reach it. This mosque has also been built by Abdul Malik. The history of this mosque can be traced all the way back to the year 536 during the reign of Emperor Justinian. On entering the mosque, one is in a large hall about hundred feet square with galleries all around. A large stone can be seen on the far wall. This historical stone contains the imprint of a foot that has been carefully preserved. The two stone pillars placed next to it are a curiosity for every traveller. It is said that every pilgrim has to pass between these two pillars or at least attempt to do so. If a man passes between them, he is said to go to heaven, that is, he is eligible for entry to the twelve heavens of God. But a man who cannot pass between them is considered to be a sinner in the eyes of God and will be consigned to hell. You can try your luck and find out what is in store for you–heaven or hell! Unfortunately, a very serious incident happened in this mosque in 1881 when a rather fat pilgrim tried to pass between the pillars and lost his life as he struggled to get through.

The Green Valleys of Jordan

After having seen the wonderful sights of Jerusalem, let us take the high road to Damascus. The road splits further ahead: the straight road on the left goes all the way to Jaffa, while the road on the right leads to Jericho via the Mount of Olives. As the Mount of Olives is the highest point in the region, it is quite a climb. But once you reach the top, it feels like you have reached heaven after a stint in hell. The view from the top is refreshing, and you can see all the hills of Jerusalem and its beautiful temples. If you look the other way, you can see a range of mountains. And if you look behind, you can see the still waters of the Dead Sea. From here, the road snakes through the hills for ten miles before it reaches Jericho. This entire area was captured by us after a pitched battle with the enemy. It has been rendered safe for travellers and traders who load their goods on camels and mules and fearlessly venture long distances. The only refuge for the tired traveller on this route is the river Jordan with its sweet flowing waters. During summers, the mountains of lime become very hot, making travel in this area very difficult. Travellers have to suffer a lot. As this area has an abundance of limestone, it becomes as hot as a furnace. This hill is lower than the hills of Hebrot and Judea, and is separated from them by the beautiful valley of the river Jordan. If we cross the bridge over the river and go ahead, the road climbs once more and leads all the way to As-Salt and the railway station of Amman. From there, the mountain railway goes all the way to Medina.

But hey, we are not bound for Medina and Mecca to perform the hajj. Is it proper for a soldier on the battlefront to behave like a tourist? Let's get back to camp!

THE BALKAN FRONT

16

A Call from the Balkans

After nearly one and a half years in the Middle East, it seemed that my wheel of fortune was going to spin in a different direction. One evening, I got orders from the sergeant major to report the next morning at ten o'clock outside the office of the battalion orderly with my packed kit. The second I heard this order, my heart sank. Now what was this new calamity! This order seemed rather strange to me. I could hardly sleep that night, wondering what it could be about and why I had been singled out. Though it was fairly routine for such orders to be issued in the army, I was rather perturbed. But 'an order is an order'.

A Call from the Mountainous War Zone of the Balkans

As ordered, I presented myself at the appointed place at the appointed time. I was handed over a large envelope and told that orders had been received from headquarters, transferring me to Salonika. I was to take these papers and report to Jerusalem, since my camp was then located on Nablus Road. I had to first trudge up to Jerusalem, and then cross the desert on my own and reach Al-Cantara. From there, I had to go to Port Said to catch the steamer. What a strange thing fate is! One day I am in Egypt, and the next day I find myself in Greece. And the months of arduous travel in between seem like child's play.

A City Blooms in the Desert

After a tiresome journey that stretched across many days, I landed in Al-Cantara again. But what a big surprise! Where there had been a dozen or so haphazardly erected ragtag tents, it now seemed that a city had bloomed in the sandy desert. There were thousands of tents stretching in every direction in an orderly fashion. If there was even a general hospital and a cinematograph, would they leave out the YMCA and the beer canteen? Earlier when we walked on the roads in the camp, our legs would sink up to the knees in the sand. It was an astounding sight to see them transformed into smooth surfaces. Soldiers could get running hot water in the bathrooms, and they had sinks to wash their faces in. Anything you wanted was freely available. All soldiers who were mobilized or demobilized on the Middle Eastern Front had to report at this camp. They would be based here for a few days before being sent to their respective regiments on the forward lines. But it was not as if they were idling here and having fun.

Each soldier was assigned a specific duty, but the job most in demand among the soldiers was that of a postman. Let us have a look at how the army post office works. On mail day, thousands of letters and parcels would be piled up at the post office. The mail would be sorted by the regiment and handed over to the respective postmen. The arrival of the post would be announced by a bugle. The minute a soldier heard the post bugle, he would drop anything he was doing and rush to the place where the mail was being distributed. You would find soldiers with one boot on their feet and the other in their hands, soldiers munching their food, and still others with only one cheek shaved. There would be complete silence as the eager soldiers would wait with bated breath, wondering if their names would be called out. Some would be awaiting letters from their parents, while others would be restlessly waiting for letters from their sweethearts. And the minute a soldier was handed over a love letter, what delight! Their excitement and happiness were a sight to behold. The average Tommy would gladly sacrifice anything to receive such a letter.

The condition in which the parcels were received was very pitiable. They would be battered and squashed, and their contents would be spilling out. If this was the situation at camp headquarters, what were the chances that parcels would be delivered at the front lines? And if a parcel did get delivered, it would not survive for too long. I remember an incident that happened when we had been marching all through the night. The next morning, we had collapsed in a heap when we were allowed a break. Just then, the post bugle sounded. It was as if all our tiredness was just a dream, and I was as eager as the rest of them to try my luck. After a short while, my name was called out. It was the first time that had happened. My friends cheered loudly as I had received a parcel from India. The unfortunate parcel had been in transit for over six months and was completely battered and covered in dirt, but that didn't make any difference to us. As my friends insisted, I opened it right away. The parcel contained sweets sent by my family. But were my hungry soldier friends bothered about what those sweets were and what they were made from? Anything was fair game—so why ask questions? The sweets were also covered with dust, but did that stop my dear Tommies? They just cleaned it the best they could and gobbled it all up. Within five minutes, it was as if no parcel had arrived. All that remained was a tin box that was being kicked around. It was always the practice among us to share whatever goodies we received from our families with all our friends. We eagerly looked forward to our friends receiving parcels from home. And then, there were others who offered money in exchange for anything edible.

If you were in a big camp, you could get whatever you wanted, but the situation was very different on the front lines. Often, it would be months before letters could be delivered. If this was the fate of letters, imagine what happened to parcels. The mail was delayed because it had to be transported on camelback. If the camels met with an accident en route or collapsed and died, the mail would get wet and dirty. But that was the last thing you were worried about when you were in the middle of a battle.

Leaving Egypt

After one final goodbye to the big encampment in Egypt, I was now off to the war zone where the final battles that decided the fate of the Great War were fought. When I was in London, I often used to hear that the British Army was having a fun time in Greece, while the soldiers fighting the war at other fronts had the worst of it. This once led to a major scuffle at the famous Victoria railway station of London, which ended in a gunfight. A few soldiers who were on leave from France encountered a group of soldiers who had arrived from Greece. The former began to banter with the latter about their easy postings. One thing led to another, and they began firing at each other, and some of them lost their lives.

However, during the final battle, it was the courageous soldiers on the Balkan Front who routed the enemy, and after many years of setbacks, scored a victory for our forces which proved to be a turning point in the Great War. I also had the opportunity to experience the battlefields of Salonika. When I received my final transfer orders from Egypt to Salonika on the 15th of May 1918, the Tommies in my platoon scared me a lot. Apparently, more soldiers were dying in Salonika because of disease than they were on the battlefield. I was quite frightened by the prospect of going to Greece.

The train from Al-Cantara to Port Said ran along the beautiful Suez Canal. At Port Said, a special steamer was waiting for us. Along with British soldiers, Indian soldiers who had recently arrived from Hindustan were also going to travel on the same ship. Besides, there were Greek soldiers on the Greek vessel. We would get our food cooked by the British cooks on board, while the Indian soldiers would have to make their own rotis. Although the voyage was pleasant, we did not have it easy. We had been drafted to train the fresh Indian recruits. The busy schedule included morning and afternoon exercise sessions. We seemed to be perpetually hungry after all the running around. However, the poor Indian soldiers could barely eat anything and just plonked themselves on the deck. They seemed to think that the sea was very rough. Their condition was very pitiable, but is there such a thing as pity in the army? There is no point in hoping for it. The tiresome journey finally came to an end when we were ordered to get ready for disembarkation two hours before we expected to dock at the harbour in Salonika. To add insult to injury, we were ordered to march to our camp as soon as we landed. We had to march five miles to general base where the Salonika camp was located.

The Huge British Camp at Salonika

Just as we alighted from the steamer, it began to rain. It was as if the clouds were waiting to welcome us. Only if you have experienced the Greek city of Salonika first-hand would you have any idea about its climate and the amount of dust in its air. Within a short while, it began to pour heavily. The rain was accompanied by a lot of lightning and thunder. The sound was enough to split our eardrums. The wind was blowing so ferociously that it seemed it would uproot all the tents. Because of the speed of the wind at Salonika, the tents had to be anchored by special pegs which were two feet long. The ordinary short pegs would just not do here. But during extreme weather, even these long pegs were of no use. We were hardly able to sleep as we were constantly worried that the tents would get uprooted. In spite of the best precautions, the tents would often get blown away.

I remember one miserable night when we were camped at Janes. As it was extremely cold, I had fashioned a small heater out of a tin box by burning a few pieces of coal in it to keep me warm at night. Thanks to the warmth, I fell into a deep sleep. It never occurred to me that we might have a thunderstorm that night. A little after midnight, I woke up with a start because of the noise. As I moved my hand to the right, I let out an involuntary shriek. My hand had been burnt by a piece of smouldering coal. The quilt on my bed was singed and smoking. A furious storm was raging outside, and the tent was teetering from side to side because of the wind. The ropes which held the tent down had snapped and were fluttering in the wind. A gust had toppled my makeshift heater and was the cause of all my problems. Where it had been burnt, the skin on my hand had turned white and was hurting badly. But I had to tackle the bigger problem first. The tent was likely to collapse at any moment. After muttering a few prayers, I ventured outside into the dark night and raging storm, and after struggling for two hours, managed to secure my tent. These kinds of problems were an everyday occurrence on the Balkan front lines. Is there any point in complaining about them now? Let's get back on the road.

We started marching in small groups towards the big encampment at Salonika. The road was quite mountainous, and we finally reached our camp at six o'clock in the evening. Row upon row of tents stretched as far as one could see. The camp at Salonika was the largest military camp in the Balkan theatre of war. Besides tents, little wooden huts had been constructed for housing the soldiers. Just next to these huts, a large battalion of soldiers was arrayed in full uniform and was waiting for marching orders to proceed to the front lines. They presented a rather curious sight. A white sack containing iron rations was hanging from the backpack of every soldier. From a distance, it seemed like they were a group of white cranes. Before being dispatched to the front lines, every soldier was provided with rations wrapped inside a white sack, which would last him twenty-four hours. The sack contained a packet of hard biscuits, a tin of bully beef, and two paper sachets of tea and sugar in another tin box. This was the reserved ration that was not supposed to be touched by the soldier unless ordered by his commanding officer. It was meant to be used only when there was a major crisis. The sack was always a test for soldiers. When they were desperately hungry, they were sorely tempted to open the sack and gobble a few biscuits. However, they never actually did so as these rations were also inspected every week. If anything was missing during the inspection, the soldier would get reported to the commanding officer and he could expect a stiff punishment. The soldiers, therefore, had to be very careful about protecting these rations.

When we saw this unit getting ready to depart for the front lines, our hearts sank to our boots. In a couple of days, it would be our turn to go to that dreaded place. Any soldier who arrived at Salonika could expect to go to the front lines in a matter of days. The arrival of every reporting soldier would first be registered at this camp, and he would then be sent to one of the numerous battlefronts. A few lucky soldiers could expect to spend a week at this camp while the unlucky ones could be dispatched immediately. It just depended on your luck.

Entertainment on the Balkan Mountains

If there had been no sources of amusement and recreation on these battlefields, the soldiers would have been left half deranged. We must thank the YMCA for having taken on this responsibility during the Great War. The YMCA had established a centre in the city of Salonika. In this country, you would never be able to find an Irani restaurant even if you searched every street. Nor could the soldiers enter the large resplendent hotels as they were 'out of bounds' for them. Where were they to go then? They could only afford to go to the YMCA where they could eat to their stomach's fill for very little money. However, military rules were applicable within the YMCA too. Even before you entered the place, a dour-looking military policeman would examine your pass to check if you had permission to venture into town. After having passed this examination, you would have to approach the counter on which a large board was placed. All the items available that day along with their prices were listed on the board. You would have to choose and pay at this counter and receive a token in return. The token would then have to be presented at the opposite counter where you could pick up the food. After having had the meal, you could go into the reading room, perhaps read for a while or write a few letters. On many evenings, an entertainment programme would be organized for the soldiers which they could watch for free. Special concert parties or orchestras would be invited from afar to entertain the soldiers. And on other days, every platoon would organize its own concert party and put up an impressive show. The divisional concert parties were a lot of fun, and both officers and soldiers had a great time. As the props and costumes for these parties were financed by the battalion fund, there never seemed to be any shortage of money. This fund tried its very best to furnish the soldiers with whatever they needed to put up a good show.

And could a large encampment like Salonika be without soap or coffee? Or beer? If the soldiers did not get their beer, their throats would be parched. As evening fell, the soldiers would promptly line up with their mess tins for their drink. It is not as if we could drink as much as we wanted. A soldier was entitled to just one pint of beer and he had to have bought a ticket earlier. If he did not have a beer ticket, he would not get a drop even if he offered to pay cash. But on the front lines, even this pint of beer was sometimes not available. However, rum was offered free of cost to the soldiers. Sometimes it would be distributed twice a week, while at other times you could get it four times a week.

17

Off to the Front Lines

Quick march! Would the army allow a soldier to spend more than a few days having fun in a city like Salonika? But then, was this city so attractive after all? All the streets were unevenly paved with stone and most were steep inclines. When you walked in Salonika in your army-issue boots, you were bound to slip and fall quite a few times, bruising your nose often. Except for the four main roads, everywhere else was a mess. Many of the streets stank so badly that you could not walk on them without holding your kerchief to your nose. You could go for a pleasant walk only on the main road which had the shops, and the road with the tramlines which skirted the ocean. If you went to the promenade to hear the Greek band, you could see the local girls walking hand in hand with the Greek soldiers. This caused a lot of heartache among us British Tommies! Was it any wonder that Salonika was not a particular favourite and we did not particularly regret leaving it when it was our turn to head to the battlefront?

Trouble on the Balkan Mountains

Once orders were issued in the morning, the soldiers had to pack up their kits and assemble on the parade ground by six o'clock in the evening and await marching orders. It is not as if the soldiers were eagerly looking forward to these orders, but there was no question of disobeying them. All of us got our kits together, including the white sack containing the iron rations which hung from our shoulders. Here, we were split into smaller groups as each group was to proceed to a different location. These groups were then ordered to march to the station where a special train was waiting. Once everybody was allocated seats according to their ranks, the soldiers could sit back and wonder about their fate. Letting out a frightening shriek of a whistle, the train began to wend its way along the mountainous tracks which snaked up the Balkans. The night journey was very tiresome, and at about seven in the morning, our group was ordered to alight at the Janes railway station. This group was made up of a mixture of soldiers from a variety of regiments, and this created a lot of problems. The station at Janes was just a halting point and nothing else. The other groups were to proceed further ahead. It was just our luck that our journey had ended at this point.

We were now ordered to report to the camps of our respective regiments. We had to find the way to these camps ourselves in ones or twos, and there was no one to guide or supervise us. Hauling our old kitbags on to our shoulders, we began to walk on those mountainous roads. Our camp was based at the foot of some hill or the other. Wherever we looked, we could only see craggy hillsides. Compared to these steeply inclined roads, the sandy roads of Egypt on which we could hardly walk seemed to be welcoming. Since we had to walk with our entire kits on these steep paths, many of the weaker soldiers just collapsed by the roadside. However, there was no one to even pity them, much less help them. And it was just our bad luck–perhaps a cat had cut across our path early in the morning–that we got lost. We roamed aimlessly for a couple of hours on those mountain paths. If we happened to meet a soldier and ask him the way to our camp, he would point to a rock face in the distance and say that if we turned left there, we would reach our camp in two minutes. Instead of two minutes, we walked for two hours, but the camp was nowhere in sight. Having left the station at seven in the morning and roamed all over the countryside, we spotted a large camp a little after nine. It must have been my lucky day as this was the camp where I was supposed to report. The others had to go further ahead to find their camps. The poor dears walked on, mumbling and grumbling.

I finally lowered the heavy load off my shoulders and presented myself at the tent of the commanding officer. As I was a complete stranger to this regiment, I became the centre of attraction. Before anybody could ask me any questions, I heard a stentorian voice asking me to 'come in'. I marched inside and presented a smart salute to the commanding officer. Luckily, this officer was very nice to me and asked me how I was doing. He also asked me where I stayed in Hindustan. But before I could answer the question, the very thought of my dear Navsari brought a few unbidden tears to my eyes. After such a terrible journey, the mere mention of my native town made me very emotional.

The Terrible State of Injured Soldiers in the Balkans

I was no longer going to face the enemy on the front lines with a gun in my hand. Nor was I going to be cooped up in a trench for days on end, wondering when the enemy would suddenly jump in. I was now going to be attached to the 31st Casualty Clearing Station (CCS), where I was going to tend to injured soldiers. From being a soldier with a gun, I was now transformed into a doctor without a licence. This hospital had two sections: one half for British soldiers and the other half for Indian soldiers. The situation was very tense in the Balkans, and a very strong offensive had been mounted on the enemy. There was always a strong likelihood of the hospital overflowing with casualties from the front lines. Injured soldiers would be brought to the CCS in field ambulances from various spots on the front lines early in the morning or at night. The receiving room of the CCS was perpetually full of stretchers, with soldiers lying on them. Some of them would be groaning in pain while others would be shrieking in fright. Many would die before they could be attended to. The pitiable situation in the hospital was enough to shake up even the most stone-hearted man.

All through the night, the injured soldiers would be operated on to remove bullets from their body or to extract fragments of iron from cannon shots. Sometimes they would have to amputate half a hand or even extract the eyeballs of an unfortunate soul. All kinds of scary procedures would be carried out from eight in the night until four or five the next morning. Some soldiers would be sent on to the main hospital without any treatment. Ill or injured soldiers would be forwarded every day from the CCS to the main hospital. As the inflow of patients was very heavy, the CCS could not afford to keep anybody a moment longer than was necessary. Two Red Cross trains ran to Salonika, one in the morning and the other in the evening, and they would be full of injured soldiers who were transferred to the custody of the medical department. These trains had special sleeper arrangements for those soldiers who were seriously injured and could not even move on their own. The medical officers would evaluate the condition of every soldier before he was evacuated. If he could not travel in a sitting position, his card would be marked as a 'lying case' and suitable arrangements would be made for him. On the other hand, if he could travel in a sitting position, he would be marked as a 'sitting case'. These medical cards were very important and would contain all the information relating to the injured soldier, including his name, his regiment, and the nature of his medical complaint. After being transported on the Red Cross train, further treatment at the main hospital in Salonika would be based on the remarks on this medical card.

18

The Final Battle

Dame fortune! It is said that nations, like humans, are born with their fate and fortune written in stone. The unfortunate Balkan region seems to have been born with a unique fate. Though it is a tiny region, it has influenced the workings of the world more than one can imagine. Just as parents find themselves drawn into a big fight when their children bicker, infighting among the Balkan states drew the powerful nations of the world into a pointless war that has resulted in a great loss of human life and endangered global stability. It is said that Karl, the emperor of Austria, regretted the fact that his country was the first to jump into the fray until his dying moment. Such is fate! But it was the same fate which ordained that a decisive victory in the Balkans would signal the end of the Great War.

The British Army played a major role in ensuring victory in the Balkan theatre. In spite of having to face immense hardships, our valorous soldiers managed to turn their losses into victory and demonstrated what an important role military discipline plays in the fortunes of an army. This victory can be largely credited to the discipline of the British soldier who, in the face of insurmountable difficulties, was willing to carry out every order that was issued by the organization. If our soldiers had disregarded any of the orders that were issued on the battlefront and had behaved as they pleased, we would never have been able to win this war. Many soldiers had been posted in the inhospitable mountains of the Balkans for three or four years. They could well have lost their nerve, but they were steadfast in their resolve. It was this resolve that was transformed into victory. I have been associated with soldiers for a long time, and I have noticed that on many occasions they would lose their patience and exclaim about the futility of the war and abuse their officers. They would even think of absconding from their posts. However, when any orders were issued, the very same soldiers would be the most mindful of them. When they set off to fight on the front lines, all such negative thoughts would be banished from their hearts. They would fight on the battlefront with true military spirit. When you consider the strong defensive fortifications that had been erected in the Balkan mountains, it was a tough job to dislodge the enemy. Storming the fortifications of the Rupal Pass in the Balkans was as tough as the Dardanelles campaign, and it was done with a major loss of life on both sides. This difficult task was undertaken slowly but surely by the French and Serbian forces, who launched an offensive east of Monastir, while the British and Greek armies advanced from Dorian. The enemy was cornered and their defences were in tatters. As they hardly had any reserve forces to reinforce the army on the front lines, their position had become indefensible. If this major offensive had been launched about ten or fifteen days later, the outcome of the war might have been different. An entire German division was on its way to the Balkan front lines, and it would have reached there in a week's time. However, it was still en route when the offensive was launched. If the Germans had been able to reinforce the enemy positions in time, it is possible that the Great War might have taken on a different colour.

German Soldiers and German Guns

They might be our enemies, but let us take a look at who the Germans are and how they fare on the battlefield. If a white officer is given charge of Indian soldiers, he typically makes a deep impression on the men and instills a sense of discipline in them. Similarly, if ten German soldiers join the combined forces of the enemy, it is as if they have been reinforced by a hundred men. I had first-hand experience of their immense courage when I was in France. During the fighting in the trenches, the Germans would hold on to their position as if they were embedded in the trench. I have seen them stick to their posts until the final minute. A German machine gunner refused to withdraw from his position even when the enemy was literally next to him. But when he finally realized the futility of fighting on, he did not simply hand over his gun. Instead, he first broke it into two, and then raised his hands calmly and surrendered. Sometimes, even when they have raised their hands, they look around to check if there is still any chance of escape with the help of their colleagues. And if, by chance, he spots them in the vicinity, he immediately seizes the opportunity! He will fish out a strategically hidden hand grenade, and suddenly the positions will be reversed. When one is trying to capture a German soldier, one has to be very careful and check all his pockets.

The trenches abandoned by the Germans were also dangerous places. Before withdrawing, they would booby-trap the trenches by placing small bombs at various locations within them. They would be hidden so skilfully that we could never spot them.

If you accidentally placed your foot on one, it would explode with disastrous consequences. At least a couple of our soldiers would be injured if they did not suffer a worse fate. These bombs would explode even if you handled them carefully. These incidents had become so routine that we would examine the trenches from a distance or throw a stone to check if a bomb exploded. Or else it might be our death warrant.

In spite of all these risks, we could never resist the temptation to examine a German gun. Just as the German cannons had acquired a reputation, these German rifles were also pretty good. During the trench warfare in France, the trenches would be soggy with water and mud. If you rested your rifle on the floor, it would begin to rot and rust. It was not a surprise that these rifles did not work quite often. Even if you cleaned the British rifles a thousand times during the day, they would still begin to rust and would not fire just when you most needed them to. But the Germans rifles were altogether special. Even if they were covered in mud or lying in water, it made no difference to them. They would neither rust nor malfunction. These rifles were longer than the British ones.

German Equipment and Uniform

We have seen that there is a lot about the Germans that is worth emulating. The equipment of the German soldiers does catch our attention. The packs which they carry on their backs are a greatly improved version of our bags. They are large enough to carry their entire household chattel. You can stuff them as much as you want. The German backpack has a leather strap on the outside. You can securely tie your folded overcoat to this strap, while we have to stuff our overcoats inside our bags, blocking over half the space inside. Similarly, these German bags have an arrangement so that the spare boots can be tied to the outside. Because of these improvements, the soldiers can pack their personal belongings inside the bag.

The equipment most worthy of praise is the German gas mask. I have already described the gas masks we used to wear on the French battlefields to protect ourselves from poisonous gases. This mask completely enclosed the head and covered both the front and the back. A rubber tube for breathing had to be permanently inserted inside the mouth. We had to do all our work with this tube in the mouth. But the German masks are completely different. They are an amazing thing. Neither is the head completely enclosed, nor does the soldier have to chew on a tube all the time. It is very easy to wear this mask, which covers only the front of the face up to the chin. There is a net impregnated with chemicals in front of the mouth. The net permits the exhalation of air, but it is so designed that it does not let the poisonous air inside. Similarly, it has glasses placed just before the eyes, which fit perfectly. There is no need for any adjustment. If you feel like it, you can keep this mask on all the time and it will not bother you. Nor does it smell of chemicals. On the other hand, the stench of chemicals that emanated from our masks was unbearable. Besides this ever-present stink, having the rubber hose in your mouth all the time was very irritating. As if this was not enough, the eyeglasses would keep slipping down. Our soldiers found this mask very irksome. Much later, our army also adopted the German design and made masks from rubber. But they had one major drawback. The air that was exhaled immediately fogged the glasses and you could not see a thing. So the rubber hose through which one breathed had to be first inserted in the mouth before wearing the mask. Even in this new design, the hose had to be always kept in the mouth, which was again a source of irritation.

The Mad Revelry of Soldiers

Victory! Victory!! Victory!!!

This was the only word on the lips of all the Tommies. The day victory was finally achieved proved to be a blessing for the soldiers, who were tired and angry after many years of prolonged conflict. As long as I am alive, I will never forget the day the confirmed news of our triumph reached our camp. It was evening when the buglers, with their gleaming bugles, began to spread all over the camp. In a short while, they began playing the tune that ordered the entire camp to assemble immediately. When the non-commissioned officers began shouting orders of 'On parade', everybody was a little worried. The camp commanding officer was himself going to be present at this parade. The other officers were also running helter-skelter. When the commanding officer himself officially announced our victory, it was as if the soldiers went crazy. Just like in our camp, we could hear loud cheers celebrating our victory from all the neighbouring camps. An impromptu band, with instruments fashioned from tin boxes and wooden containers, began playing. Soldiers were enjoying themselves by flinging empty beer bottles in the air which added to the music as they crashed to the ground. The soldiers had already begun to make plans to have a huge show of fireworks. You can well imagine the revelry that resounded all through the night.

The soldiers gathered as much wood as they could, and lit a huge bonfire and danced around it. It reminded me of the night of Holi. They did not leave out the empty tents, and gathered as many of them as they could and burnt them too. A few mischievous soldiers even managed to get boxes of bullets and threw them into the bonfire. The bullets began to explode like crackers. It was mayhem everywhere. Nobody bothered about rules or regulations. It was as if the soldiers had free rein. After years of misery and hardship, everybody was looking forward to returning home as soon as possible. We have already seen that it was the disturbances in the Balkans which drew the entire world into this war. And it was peace in the Balkans which signalled the end of the Great War.

The big military camp at Salonika was no longer necessary, and it was slowly wound up and moved elsewhere. I was assigned duties to help in winding up the hospital. Three months after the victory, we received orders to advance towards the world-famous city of Constantinople, the capital of Turkey. From Salonika, we boarded the steamer *Australian* and advanced towards the Black Sea.

AFTER THE TRUCE

19

Georgia

We did not stop at Constantinople but pressed on towards Georgia. I promised myself that I would be back to take a proper look at this historic city.

Trains on the Caucasus Mountains

As we have already seen above, the world is full of places with beautiful monuments and breathtaking natural scenery. One such place is the world-famous city of Tiflis, the capital of Georgia, which brings to mind its ancient culture. This unfortunate city has presently fallen by the wayside and is ignored by everyone. Our rich Indians make a beeline for vilayat and consider it to be the acme of civilization. They are unable to appreciate the beauty of cities such as Tiflis, and visiting historical places seems to tire them out. When I was younger, I had read stories of 'Layla and the Magical Garden', but never had I imagined that I would be able to see such a magical place myself. Travelling in the Caucasus mountains with their frightening peaks was an altogether special experience.

To reach Tiflis, one has to cross the Black Sea and alight from the steamer at Batumi which has a beautiful harbour. Bidding a final goodbye to Batumi, one has to travel a distance of about 250 miles by train. It is quite a scary journey as the railway track climbs up the steep Caucasus mountains. The comfortable trains of the Trans-Caucasus Railway, which depart from Batumi, take us all the way to the Caspian Sea where the line terminates at Baku. There are quite a few trains departing from Batumi. Evidently, it is not an insignificant city and is home to a variety of communities. A similar variety can be seen in the languages spoken in Batumi. It seems to be a mixture of a little Turkish, a little Russian, and bits of Gurjansky. If you know Russian, you will face no problems here. If not Russian, then French will take you a long way; or else you might stick out like a sore thumb. Kerosene is the most important product of trade in this country. The oil is transported from Baku in tanks and offloaded on to steamers at Batumi and exported all over the world. Oil is so cheap in this country that even the engines that haul trains have been modified so that oil can be used instead of coal. A tank is constructed above the coal storage area behind the engine to store the oil. Water is stored in the water tank as usual. The oil is conveyed through a pipe to the engine where it is burnt as usual. No need for the engine driver to be plastered in black dust.

We travelled by a troop train from Batumi and had the entire train to ourselves. As it made its way up the Caucasus mountains, a strange atmosphere of fear took hold. The more the train ascended, the more our hearts fell. The mountain peaks were so high and scraggy, it seemed that they might topple over one another at any moment. From a distance, it seemed that many of the mountaintops were hanging on precariously. In certain stretches, it seemed that the vibrations of the train would cause the mountains to come tumbling down and crush our train. I involuntarily muttered the 'Yatha Ahuvairyo' a few times when we passed such places. In spite of such dangers, our dear train slithered like a snake through the mountain passes and we had a good time of it. The two engines attached to the front and the back of the train created such a racket that it dispelled all our fears.

The Tiflis Railway Station

Our troop train screeched to a halt at the railway station in Tiflis. The platform was swarming with Georgian soldiers. In fact, there were more soldiers than there were passengers. The very sight of them—with their yard-long hats and guns with long bayonets—was enough to inspire awe in any bystander. And they had the attitude to match their looks. If anybody got into an argument with them, they were quite willing to use their guns. However, they behaved quite decently with visitors like us and were willing to run errands for us in the hope of a small tip. If we were in a generous mood and gave them a packet of cigarettes which cost a mere three annas, their faces would light up with joy.

There were a few local Georgians at the station and they reminded me of our Indian villagers. Wonder why they were aimlessly running around the station with their bundles of cloth on their heads? The station is certainly big enough to get lost in. If you climb the stairs up one platform to go to an office on another platform, you may not be able to find your way back. And if you do not know the Gurjansky language, you will find yourself in a spot. Nobody here can speak a word of English to save themselves. But once you have learnt their language, this country is one of the best places in Europe. They do not discriminate based on colour or caste. It does not matter if you are black or white or from a high or low caste. Everybody is treated just the same.

Currency Exchange Rate Issues

When you step out of the grand Tiflis station, you will find horse carts hauled by two horses waiting to take you around the city. If you know exactly which hotel you want to go to, you will have no problems, but if you have no specific destination, you will be in trouble. It takes a lot of effort to make these cart drivers understand where you want to go. In fact, the language problem was worse than what I had faced in China. But there was a bigger problem waiting for me. The currency used in Tiflis is the Russian rouble, and they will not accept even the rouble that is in circulation in Batumi or Baku. They may still be accepted in the larger shops and the currency exchanges, but the labouring classes refuse to touch them. The exchange rate fluctuates so wildly that you are bound to book a loss. A guinea might fetch you three hundred roubles today and perhaps five hundred tomorrow. If you want to purchase anything in Tiflis, you had better be prepared to take a hit, like it happened to me. You might say, 'Not again!'

But why not travel to this city that is situated between the Caspian Sea and the Black Sea in the western parts of Asian Russia and south of the Caucasus? This city was important enough to catch the attention of Emperor Heraclius. He mounted a campaign in 626 to conquer it from the Iranians. However, according to history, he had to face defeat at their hands. The beautiful city of Tiflis is situated at a height of 1,800 feet in the Caucasus mountains at the mouth of the river Kur. The meaning of the word 'tiflis' is 'hot'. Just like in our country, there are quite a few hot springs surrounding this city. As the temperature of the city is very high during the summers, it acquired the name of Tiflis, that is, the 'hot city'. And similarly, this region has been named the Caucasus after the Caucasus mountains. The weather in the plateau region to the north is cold, like in European Russia, but the southern parts are very fertile, where a variety of fruits are cultivated. It is said that this tiny country has a population made up of over 150 nationalities. Over seventy different languages are spoken here. Before the Great War, the population of the city was about 200,000. Just like its weather, the prices here seem to be hot. And even the people here are rather hot-headed. If you go on a stroll with a lady in Tiflis, you better steer clear of a florist. The people here seem to be crazy about chocolate. If you go into a chocolatier's, you will be poorer by a hundred roubles at least. The salesgirls who work in these shops encourage you to purchase more than you intend to. When you enter the shop, a couple of girls come running to welcome you with flashing smiles. If you ask for something, they will present you with fifty choices. And there is no question of haggling. You have to silently pay up whatever is demanded, or else your lady companion might get annoyed by your lack of etiquette. As each product has labels indicating its price, there is really no question of haggling over it. Russian sweets are available cheaply, but French chocolate is rather expensive, and a person like me cannot stomach paying fifty roubles for a bit of chocolate. In those days, the rouble was becoming stronger and you could only get eighty roubles for a guinea. A packet of chocolate cost the equivalent of our six rupees. The exchange rate fluctuated wildly, and everything had become so expensive that a person like me could hardly afford anything. The locals had to cough up 100–150 roubles for an ordinary loaf of bread! The prices may have risen by a factor of three by now. Even the ladies have to labour very hard under these circumstances. Wherever you go, you can see women working. But at the same time, the people here do not miss out on having fun when they can. After having worked hard the whole day, you can see them meeting their friends in the evening to have a good time.

Flowers on a Sunday

The city of Tiflis seems to be full of strange and wonderful things. One such wonder is its flowers. To walk with a bouquet of sweet-smelling flowers is considered up-to-date fashion in Tiflis. You might even say that the practice has reached epidemic proportions. Men insert flowers in the buttonholes of their coats, but women take it to extremes, especially on Saturdays and Sundays. It seems that a woman's entire costume is plastered with roses from head to toe. A bunch of flowers is sure to hang down her chest. A few roses are tucked into the belt around her waist. And why leave out the belt? Roses dangle from its two ends. She has a bouquet of violet flowers in her hand. When you spend an evening with a lady, and if she does not have a bouquet, you are expected to buy her one to keep up appearances, or else you will be the laughing stock of town because you did not understand their etiquette. This is bound to empty your wallet. All the major roads are dotted with shops which display flowers for sale in baskets. The price could range from twenty to forty roubles, depending on what kind of flower it is and who the buyer is. Such are the practices in different countries.

Open-Air Theatre

Tiflis! Long may your glories survive! Though Tiflis is a very colourful city, its residents can be quite eccentric and often behave strangely. During the summers, the mountains surrounding the city trap the heat and make life miserable for its citizens. After having worked hard the whole day, they would go crazy if they had to spend their evenings shut up in their houses. Rather than staying at home, they prefer to step out. In the hot season, cinematographs without roofs are specially built to screen films.

Many of these theatres have cafes attached to them. Patrons can sip on their favourite drinks while watching the cinematograph. After dinner, people step out to stroll in the public gardens which are open till late. In these gardens, bands play music well into the wee hours. Sometimes, there are five or six bands playing in a single garden. All kinds of light refreshments—ice cream soda, lemonade, tea—are available. All you need is money to spend. You can spot groups of rosy-cheeked Circassian beauties in flimsy white garments frolicking with their friends. The passing traveller can only marvel at their beauty.

Sword Dance of Circassian Soldiers

The uniform of the Georgian soldiers is just as strange as the nature of its people. Ignorant travellers like me are taken aback by the costume of their military officers. It is not that their uniform is stitched from expensive cloth, but it is the embellishments and ornamentations that seem rather weird and over the top. The breeches of the uniform are extremely tight around the calves and are enclosed in knee-high black boots. A large overcoat is worn over a very tight chemise. From their cummerbund hangs a heavy metal sword. Besides a double-edged dagger that is tucked into the cummerbund, they carry yet another smaller dagger with them. They also have a big pistol whose cartridges are inserted in a series of tiny chest pockets. Needless to add, further decoration is provided by the medals hanging from their chest. Their long moustaches twirled up into fine points and their ruddy faces are enough to complete the ensemble—quite a scary sight to be sure!

They are highly skilled swordsmen and their sword dance is quite a speciality. It does seem that soldiers from this region are rather obsessed with their swords. If a couple of soldiers get into an argument, it does not take long for them to draw swords. Such incidents are quite common after they have had a drink or two. They seem to get into the spirit of the sword dance after a few pegs of vodka and put up quite a performance. Two long swords are placed on the ground to form a cross. A man and a woman step up to the sound of music. They stand facing each other and begin dancing. What is their objective? The man has to catch the woman without disturbing the swords. If his foot touches the swords, he is considered to have lost. After they have danced a while, the music suddenly stops playing. The two adversaries also stop dancing. This is the most critical moment as their bodies are still swinging from the momentum. It is at this time that their feet might touch the swords. The crowd also whips itself up into a frenzy and bets on the outcome as if they are betting on horses. Some of them get so worked up that occasional sword fights suddenly break out. Most people in Georgia seem to be skilled at wielding a sword. Swords and daggers in a variety of sizes with beautiful and ornamental hilts are freely available in the local markets.

A Novel Marriage in the Land of Ice

Are there any candidates for the marriage market? If yes, then let us go to the Winter Garden of Tiflis. I have seen winter gardens in vilayat and other countries, but the one in Tiflis seems to be in a class of its own. During the winters, Tiflis becomes so cold that it is impossible for its citizens to stroll along the gardens of the city. Special winter gardens are erected for the pleasure of the residents, where they can enjoy themselves. If you shell out about twenty-five roubles, you will literally be transported to heaven at the winter garden. The greenery inside these glass palaces is complemented by colourful electric lights. In this land of snow, you will also get to see snow-white beauties all decked up in their best clothes. It felt like I was in Aladdin's wonderland! When you hear the music played by the band, you are bound to feel like dancing yourself. These Circassians are better dancers than the English ladies, that is, they are as good as the French.

You should be forewarned that it is better to stay away from these places rather than make a regular habit of it. If one dances with the same partner every day, it is only a matter of time before things take a rather unexpected turn. After a short period of courtship, the girl will suggest marriage in a church. Before the wedding, the couple can agree on the duration of the marriage. You can get married for one year, and there are no restrictions on such marriages in this country. This is downright ridiculous! They seem to think of marriage as a game. What happens to the bride and groom after the agreed period is completed? I guess they can go in search of new partners. Those who contract such marriages seem to be labouring under a delusion. It is best for us Parsis to stay as far away as possible from such things.

20
Baku

Can a city just crop up in the middle of nowhere? Well, come with me and I will show you! Moving on from Tiflis, the Trans-Caucasus Railway extends for a further two hundred miles before reaching the coast of the Caspian Sea where the world-famous oil springs are located. When was I going to get another chance to see this place?

The History of Baku

The Trans-Caucasus Railway terminates at Baku. If one wants to travel further east, one can board the steamer for Krasnovodsk, the starting point for the Trans-Caspian Railway, which goes all the way to Samarkand and Bukhara. The Iranians came by the land route to conquer this city, but in 1723, the Russians snatched it from their hands. Since then, the city has frequently seen new rulers. Baku has been settled by numerous communities, including Armenians, Russians, Georgians and Azerbaijani Mohammedans. It seems that Azerbaijanis are currently the dominant community. Before the Great War, there was an Azerbaijani government at Baku, but it was reconquered by the Russian Bolsheviks during the war. Towards the end of the year 1918, our victorious forces entered the city via the Caucasus. Another army also arrived by land from Iran and the city was captured. When the British Army was withdrawn from Baku, the Azerbaijanis again took control of the city.

The city of Baku is split into two parts: the old town and the new town; the latter is growing rapidly. The old town occupies the original fort whose walls have fallen into disrepair. There used to be a palace inside this fort which was built in the sixteenth century, but even its ruins have disappeared. The roads inside the fort are very narrow, dark and dirty. However, the new town has been built in an altogether different style. Modern barracks have been constructed on the Caspian coast. The markets have large shops and restaurants that are built in the French style. Besides, there are cinematographs and an imperial theatre. The antics of the Azerbaijani soldiers and the citizens strolling on the promenade are a sight to see.

However, the situation takes on a different colour as night falls. You can hear gunshots being fired from all quarters. The residents are a scared lot and seem to be abandoning the city. Skirmishes regularly break out between the Armenians and the Azerbaijanis, and a lot of lives have been lost. If there is a little disturbance in the city, the electricity and water supplies are turned off. The residents had to live under such trying circumstances. It was only when the British government decided to take a strict stand that things were brought under control. Posters were stuck at prominent places in the city, warning of strict penalties, including hanging by death, if anybody was caught disturbing the peace. This admonition seemed to have a salutary effect. We could then go wherever we wanted to without fear.

The Jwalamukhi Near the Caspian Coast

Some might say that I am bluffing. Or a religious fanatic might come forward thumping his chest and ask me how I could write about our atashbehram like this. I am not particularly bothered about the consequences and might as well take this opportunity to drop a little note here! I think it is worth a little more investigation.

The history of Baku is not so voluminous that it would fill up a big book. It was of little account and was completely ignored by everyone until the year 1866, when it suddenly came to everybody's attention. All the great powers of the world are vying to take control of it because of the stupendous income generated by the thousands of oil wells in and around Baku. Before 1866, only a few oil springs located in the villages of Balakhaneh and Surukhaneh were known. Surukhaneh is also known as Dapu, and even the Hindus claim to exercise control over this place. The Parsis claim that there was an atashbehram in Baku, while the Hindus claim that it is their temple. It is not for someone like me to pass judgement on such matters. Next to the temple is a dharamshala, which is said to be much older than the temple as its inscriptions are completely worn out.

However, when I went to this place during my stay in Baku, all I could see was stray dogs. Neither could I see the burning fire, nor could I see the temple. It was just stone and rubble. Nor are you going to meet the officiating priest of the temple. On inquiring with the locals, I was informed that until the year 1880, the flame was tended to by a Hindu sadhu. There were other Hindus before him. In 1866, the resident priest was murdered by a Tartar who wanted to rob the temple of its riches that had been donated by pilgrims. After his death, another Hindu sadhu continued to officiate at the temple, but after 1880, the temple was abandoned. The flame, which is locally known as Jwalamukhi, has been harnessed for a different use. The spring has been sealed and the gas from the well has been put to use in a local industry. How would there be any flame now? It is said that the flame burnt eternally as it was fuelled by the gas.

A Lemon-Tea Picnic on Sunday

As the residents of Baku are inclined towards having a good time, how do you think they spend their Sundays? The working classes get paid by the week every Saturday. Once they get their salary, they buy a chunk of meat big enough to last them for the entire week and steam it. The following day, Sunday, is devoted to fun. They don their best clothes and step out of their houses. Some of them head for the church, while others plan a day trip. You can see entire families setting out for picnic parties in the morning with their food and drink. They board ferry boats and cross over to the opposite side within an hour. The wharves are decorated in bright colours and a band welcomes the arriving boats. Small groups fan out and seek the best spots under trees, where they set up camp for the entire day. What is the first thing they do once they settle down? They light a fire to boil water in a small kettle and make Russian tea. Milk and sugar are not used; instead, they put a thin slice of lime in the cup of tea. You have to sip the tea slowly and enjoy its taste. After a few sips, the slice of lime is spooned up and tasted before being slipped back into the tea. This tea drinking is a prolonged and relaxed affair. Like the Chinese, they drink tea the whole day, and wherever they go, they carry all that is necessary for tea! Each nation has its own customs. Come Monday and they revert to their usual selves and are back at work. In Europe, they have clearly specified days for fun and work. After having had a good time on Sunday, you can see the same ladies rolling up their sleeves to get on with their housework. On Monday, it is the laundry which they themselves do at home. Tuesday is devoted to cleaning the home thoroughly, while on Wednesdays, the glass panes on all the doors and windows are washed. It does not matter how educated the lady is–she could have just completed school or she could be a college graduate with a BA degree. Compared to them, our Parsi ladies are like those proverbial half-full cans that make a lot of noise. If they have acquired a few words of English, they turn up their noses and exclaim, 'What nonsense! Why should we do any housework since we are educated?' Not only do the European ladies keep track of their household chores and tick them off in their things-to-do notebook, but they also set out to work after they have done their domestic duties. After having toiled the whole day, they return home in the evening and then set out to meet friends. They are not willing to waste even one hour of the day doing nothing. Aren't they enthusiastic about life? My poor dear Hindustan, how many more centuries before you arrive at this stage?

The World-Famous Oil Wells

Of all the wondrous things in this country, the most strange and wonderful are its world-famous oil wells. In Baku, one can see oil wells by the hundreds, or rather thousands. This oil forest is located in Balakhaneh, which is about twenty miles from Baku. One can go there by rail or take a ferry boat. By rail, one has to alight at Balakhaneh station. The town is on one side of the station while the oil wells are on the other. It looks like a forest from a distance. From the station, one can walk straight towards it. One does not need a guide of any sort. However, if one wants a vehicle, horse-drawn carriages are available at the station. On entering the oil forest, all the roads are slick with oil and there is a thick layer of sludge on them. One can smell the oil everywhere. You better not wear any new clothes when you visit the place as they are bound to get coated with oil in a few minutes. The cacophony of the oil wells is enough to drive you crazy. It is too noisy to even have a conversation. But why complain about such stuff when you have gone to see one of the strangest things in the world? Before I visited this place, I used to think that these oil springs would be similar to water springs and would be flowing on the surface. But when I came here, I learnt something altogether different. In this oil forest, oil wells have been dug every ten to twenty yards. These wells are about three thousand feet deep and are topped by very expensive machinery. A triangular wooden structure has been erected atop every well, which extends to three hundred feet in height. An iron ring hangs from the apex of this structure, to which is attached a long metal wire. A hollow pipe, about fifteen feet long, is fixed to the end of the wire. This pipe has been so constructed that its bottom opens out once it touches the ground and again shuts when it is above the ground. This is the pipe that is used to extract oil from the well. Each oil well is monitored by a man who keeps a close watch on the entire process by which the pipe enters the well, fills up with a mixture of oil and water, and is again drawn up above the surface where it empties out its contents. Sometimes the water content is high, while at other times it is mainly oil. The mixture of oil and water is directed via open pipes to a location where it is collected before the oil and water are separated. The oil is collected in tanks, while the water is drained into the ocean. Some wells dry up after a lot of expense has been incurred on them, in which case the proprietor is put to great loss. It is said that thousands, or rather millions, of rupees are invested in each well. The income is proportionate to this investment, and if a man invests in three to four wells, he can expect to earn millions of rupees.

Oil is available at very cheap prices in Azerbaijan and is even used to light cooking stoves. Neither is there need to bother with the hassle of wood or cow dung, nor do the white ladies have to worry about soot blackening their faces. The mechanism is very simple and straightforward. A small tin tank is placed before the stove. The tank has two compartments: one is filled with oil and the other with water. Both compartments are fitted with taps from which pipes channel the oil and water to the stove. When the taps are opened, oil and water reach the stove and can be lit with a matchstick. Once the cooking is done, the taps can be turned off to extinguish the fire easily. It could not be simpler. You can also control the intensity of the flame by turning the tap. What kind of intelligence must have figured this out? Clearly the world is full of brains, but it is time for us to move on.

Departure from Baku

As per the latest military regulation, it was time for soldiers who had joined the army in 1914 and 1915 to discard their khaki uniform and become gentlemen again. Those soldiers who had been recruited in 1916 would have to spend two more years in the army. The date for my departure from Baku was nearing as I was stamped 'Back for Blighty'. My new-found friends shed a few tears in anticipation of our impending separation. One fine evening, I was finally served my discharge warrant, something I had never expected. Can you imagine my joy? I was excited about travelling again on the Trans-Caucasus Railway, crossing the Black Sea, and hoping to wave one final goodbye to Constantinople. And I was looking forward to going back to England via Italy and France. Even as I write this, I can recall the thrill of all those journeys and I yearn for those experiences.

21
Constantinople

O Sea Goddess! We ultimately have to find refuge in you. Our ship was now bobbing up and down in the ocean, but I had been conditioned to experience ups and downs since childhood. But right now, I was looking forward to alighting on the coast of the Bosphorus. After days of tiresome travel over open seas, it was a completely different experience as we entered the strait of Bosphorus. Those travellers–especially women and children–who had been plagued by seasickness were refreshed by the sight of the greenery along the coast. I was not able to see this tip of Asia on my way towards Salonika but had only got a faraway glimpse. I had then decided that I would certainly be back to visit this historic place. Now was my chance!

Let us take a tour around the Turkish capital of Constantinople. The views of the city as we pass along the Bosphorus are like seeing the beauty of the entire world. Indeed, there are many beautiful harbours all over the world. When I first went to Hong Kong, I was of the opinion that there was no other coast that could match up to it. But having seen Constantinople, it seems that I have to consign my opinion to the dustbin. As we sailed along the strait of Bosphorus, we could see high mountains on both sides, covered with a variety of greenery. The strong fortifications of the famous fort of Bosphorus can be seen on both sides. The mountainsides are dotted with huge cannons that seem to be intimidating the traveller. It is not as if these cannons are placed in the open. They are placed at strategic locations within the mountains in strong masonry structures. It is highly unlikely that an enemy can enter the strait of Bosphorus under the gaze of these cannons. And if any enemy vessel does venture into this strait, it is bound to be hit within minutes. There is nowhere to hide as the strait is very narrow; a thin strip between two steep mountains through which the water flows. And there is no way you can turn back either. It seems like nature has doubly blessed the Turkish nation. On one side are the natural mountainous fortifications of the Dardanelles which cannot be conquered in spite of years of war, and on the other side are the fortifications overlooking the strait of Bosphorus which guard the entrance from the Black Sea. Even the defences at the Bosphorus may be considered natural. On passing through these near-impregnable straits that have astounded even senior European generals, we could see small villages on both sides. These mountain villages have become picnic spots for the residents of Constantinople. On every Friday and Saturday, they descend in large numbers with their picnic boxes and drinks on small boats. These abandoned villages seem to have got a new lease of life and reverberate with the laughter of children and beautiful young women. It seems that the Turks who stay in Constantinople know how to enjoy life. The many streams which flow down these mountains seem to be veritable springs of nectar. Many of them reminded me of our famous hot springs. It is said that the water from these springs has medicinal properties and can stimulate one's appetite. I am told that it is filled in bottles and is sent to many parts of Europe. The world is indeed full of the most curious things. It is said that there are villages in and around Navsari where the toddy has miraculous properties and, therefore, the residents never feel like leaving the village. How would the Turkish then give up these places? It is said that even travellers do not feel like leaving this part of the world.

The Golden Horn

Believe it or not, but if you want to experience the beauty of the world from a distance, then the strait of Bosphorus is the place to be. Even the sights of vilayat would pale in comparison. It is fun to see a goggle-eyed European memsahib clap her hands as she takes in the wonderful attractions of this city and exclaims, 'How sweet!' Your first sight of the Sultan's palace, shining white on the coastline, will astound you. When you enter the palace, you are bound to say that you will be back again. But you better not forget your binoculars when you are coasting down the Bosphorus. The best way to see this Turkish city is from the sea, but it is no fun without binoculars. When you hear the white memsahibs shout out 'How nice!' as they peer through their binoculars, you are bound to feel that you are missing out on something. You might feel like snatching those binoculars from their hands.

The city is laid out on both sides of the strait, but the famous Golden Horn caught my attention first. The numerous small boats with their passengers are a delight, and the girls waving their colourful handkerchiefs seemed to be welcoming me to their country. The traveller is refreshed by these sights.

A Brief History of Constantinople

Constantinople, which is in the magnificent Islamic country of Turkey, is on the radar of many powerful countries, and the attention of the entire world is focused on it. They are wondering how to bring it under their control. This beautiful but unfortunate city seems to have always been embroiled in troubles, and they seem to persist right into the present times. This city is divided into two parts. One of them is known as Istanbul while the other is known as Galata. Before the Great War, the population of the city was estimated to have exceeded 1,200,000, but currently, it might not be even half that number. Turkey was involved in the war from the very start and is still suffering from its aftermath. It is said that this Byzantine city was founded in the year 690 BC by the Megaran king Byzas. The seraglio is said to occupy the site of that ancient city. The city later came under the control of the Persian emperor Darius. It then passed from hand to hand and fell back into ruin. If one were to describe the history of the Turkish country, it would fill up an entire book. In the Christian era, the great emperor Constantine completely changed the fortunes of this city. He has become immortal by building a new city–named Constantinople after himself–spread over seven hills. The city continued to be ruled by many different rulers, and finally, in the fifteenth century, it came under the rule of the Mohammedans. In 1453, Sultan Fateh Mehmed, son of Sultan Murad, conquered this city after a pitched battle. For the last five hundred years or so, it has remained under the control of the Mohammedans and has flourished under their care to become world-famous. Sultan Fateh Mehmed named the city Istanbul and built numerous mosques. The German emperor Kaiser William himself visited this city in 1894. This great city is split into ten divisions: Istanbul accounts for the first three divisions, while the European city sprawls over the fourth, fifth and seventh divisions. The sixth division is Galata, while the eighth division is Pera, which is behind the Asian coast of Socotra. The ninth division is Socotra itself, while the tenth and the last division is Kadikoy. The Mohammedan population seems to be mainly concentrated in Istanbul.

Having travelled thousands of miles to reach this Turkish city, it would be a crime not to saunter aimlessly on its streets. All the effort to get here would amount to nothing. Having seen the Golden Horn from the steamer, let us go on land to take a look at Constantinople. As we venture deeper into the city, it feels like we are walking along the streets of Agra or Delhi. The roads are lined with tiny shops in the Indian fashion, which are stocked with a variety of goods. You cannot help but buy something. Just like our Indian businessmen, it seems that our Turkish friends have vowed not to affix a standard price to any of their goods. If you buy anything, make sure that you negotiate sharply, or else you might be taken for a ride. On top of all this confusion, all the prices are in piastres, a currency that the traveller might not be familiar with. Before the Great War, one of our guineas was worth a hundred piastres. But presently, the exchange rate is all up in the air. It could be two hundred piastres one day and five hundred the next. This confusion is a double hit for the traveller. Everything seems to be in a state of confusion in Turkey these days; why complain only about the exchange rate?

Let us take a look around town. As we enter a narrow lane, we encounter a series of houses which seem very strange. The houses are built entirely from wood and topped with slate roofs. In each house, a window juts out from the centre of the facade. It must be dangerous to stay in such houses. All across Asia Minor, one can see houses built in this fashion. As these houses are built of wood, the probability of fire is very high. To keep such fires under control and warn the residents by promptly informing them about any conflagration, a very strange but effective system has been developed in Constantinople. If there is a fire in any locality, this information is very quickly transmitted to all of Constantinople. A very tall tower, about 550 feet high, has been built on a hill in the city. A man is always stationed on top of the tower. If he spots a fire in any part of the city, he immediately raises a flag during the day.

When I first arrived in the city and noticed a variety of flags being hoisted on the tower during the day and being replaced by coloured lights during the night, I thought that they announced the arrival and departure of steamers. I parked myself near the coast and kept scanning the horizon to see if this was indeed the case. But when there was no sign of any approaching steamer even after a flag was hoisted, I wondered what these flags and lights really signified. One night, I stood for half an hour looking at the lights being lit and extinguished, and also kept an eye out on the sea. However, when I still could not find any connection between the two, I got irritated and decided to ask around. As I did not know the Turkish language, how was I to get a reply? Only later did I find out that these flags and lights were meant to convey the news of fire in various localities. Often there would be two or three lights shining simultaneously, which meant there were that many fires raging at that moment. This tower has been constructed on the highest spot in the city and is known as the Galata Tower. It is said that this tower dates from the time of Sultan Mehmed II.

In a Turkish Cafe

In every nook and corner of the Turkish Sultanate, one can find a Turkish cafe or kawakhana. Wherever one goes, the first thing one can see is a Turkish cafe. There are cafes catering to every section of society, ranging from the uppermost classes to the poorest people. Is there anyone among our dear Turks who does not visit these cafes at least once a day and spends five to seven minutes there?

These places are indeed a blessing for the stranger, as he can get the latest news at these cafes and also observe local rites and customs. Even a poor labourer who has toiled all through the day will, come evening, go to a cafe and get himself a cup of coffee. He may sip it inside the cafe or step outside and have it by the roadside. Unless he gets his daily fix, he will not be able to sleep at night. But I must say that this Turkish coffee did not appeal to my taste. It is so bitter that it tastes like castor oil. The coffee is served in a tiny cup with no milk or sugar, but is accompanied by a big glass of cold water. It is supposed to be drunk with the coffee. Some aficionados even mix the water with the coffee and drink the mixture.

My first experience at a cafe was rather bitter. I was feeling tired after walking and thought that I might as well relax inside one. Just as I sat down at a table, the Turkish head waiter appeared by my side, and greeting me with a deep bow, asked, 'Cafe, Monsieur?' I answered 'Yes!' with a flourish. In a few moments, a large tray was placed in front of me. The coffee was served in a tiny cup and saucer, the kind children play with. A large tumbler of water was also placed next to it. I was rather perplexed when I saw this tiny cup; I could have fifty of them and would still not be satisfied. But wait! When I had the first sip, I realized my mistake as I could barely swallow this coffee. It was altogether too strong and just as bitter. Each drop of coffee made me want to vomit, but what was I to do? Having ordered the coffee, I felt obliged to drink it. I decided to drain the cup in one go, but when I did that, huge teardrops trickled from my eyes. But this was not the end of my troubles. As they say, dangers come in pairs. I still had one more waiting for me. I assumed that the large glass of water was for washing up and inserted my fingers in it and began to wash my hands. As I was doing this, the adjoining table burst into laughter. It seemed that practically everyone at the cafe was staring and laughing at me.

I was mightily embarrassed, but what could be done now? I was so irritated that I could have got up and hammered all of them. The strange customs of strange countries are bound to trip up the traveller, but one has to take it in one's stride. I thought that the glass was for washing up as it was filled to the brim, but only found out later that it had to be sipped alternately with the coffee. Only if one sip of coffee is followed by a mouthful of water can this drink be enjoyed. Along with this famed coffee, a hookah seems to be mandatory. Connoisseurs contend that drinking coffee is not worth it without a hookah. You may not believe it, but all kinds of intoxicants are available at some cafes. Besides, many of them have dancing girls to entertain you. These Egyptian and Turkish dances are certainly worth a look. But you better be extremely careful before venturing into such places. There is a probability that you might not come back alive.

There are people loitering on the streets of Constantinople who claim to be guides and offer to give you a tour of the city. The traveller should think twice before engaging one of them. They might take you to an isolated place, and not only lighten your wallet but also beat you to a pulp.

There are over three hundred takiyas or rest houses for travelling fakirs in this city. These places also serve as refuge for homeless people. As some of these takiyas also serve food for free, they attract a lot of poor fakirs. The Turkish people have a lot of respect for these fakirs and think it a blessing to serve them. It is very rare for one of them to go hungry. These rest houses also have mosques within their premises that are beautifully decorated. Each mosque seems to be more attractive than the next. Can you guess the number of mosques in Constantinople? It is estimated that there are about five hundred mosques in the city.

The Famous Mosque of Hagia Sophia

Where should you go if you want to see mosques? Obviously Constantinople! Of the numerous mosques in the city, the most impressive one is the Hagia Sophia, which is considered to be one of the oldest monuments of the world. I do not have words to describe its grandeur. Just like this city itself, this monument has seen many ups and downs as it passed under the control of a series of rulers. In the year 336, the emperor Constantine had used it as a Christian temple. After that, it passed through a series of disasters and was even burnt down once. It was rebuilt in 532 by Emperor Justinian. But, as they say, the wheel of fortune keeps turning, and what was once an ancient church passed into the hands of the Mohammedans. It was converted into a mosque in 1453 after the establishment of the power of Sultan Fateh Mehmed. For nearly five hundred years, it has been used by millions of Muslims as a house of prayer.

One can get an idea about the scale of this monument by the fact that when it was being constructed, layouts of ancient Egyptian and Greek monuments had been requisitioned. It was built over a period of many years by thousands of labourers under the supervision of a hundred engineers. It is estimated that about fifteen million rupees were expended on its construction. When we look at this famous mosque from a distance, we can get a feel of its antiquity. The central dome and the four beautiful minarets present a beautiful vista from a distance. The history of these minarets is also interesting. The first minaret is said to have been built by Sultan Mehmed II, while the next two were built by Sultan Murad III. The beautiful workmanship on these minarets leaves the traveller spellbound. With great difficulty, he turns his gaze away from them and enters the huge courtyard of the mosque, where he has to leave his boots behind according to the Mohammedan custom. Ah! As he steps inside the mosque, he cannot but exclaim in delight when he sees the splendorous interiors. The marble columns, the intricately designed arches, and the golden-hued viewing galleries dazzle his eyes. He is flummoxed by all the wondrous objects and cannot decide where to start. He feels like taking it all in at one go. The vastness of the interior can be gauged by the dimensions of the central hall. It is about 270 feet long and 245 feet wide. On entering the hall, we can see that it has been split into three wings. Both the wings on the left and right contain four columns of green marble, mounted by five arches, which in turn support the six arches that hold up the roof. The circular gallery in the hall is a good example of Italian workmanship. It is great fun to climb up to the gallery and gaze down at the wonders of this mosque. The gallery reminds us of St Paul's Church in London. When we come down again and look up at the dome, we are filled with fright. How has this huge dome, under which thousands of people can stand, been erected?

An Underground Lake

Does even God know all the wonderful things that are hidden in the continent of Asia? We live in a godforsaken corner of the world. How are we to imagine the strange and mysterious things which exist elsewhere? Only when we get an opportunity to roam the world and see its amazing sights do we realize what we were missing. Although I had seen innumerable monuments in Asia, I was dazzled by the sight of the minarets of the Hagia Sophia. As I came up to the site of an underground lake known as the Cistern, I had no clue what this place might contain. The first thought that occurred to me was: 'What is there to see in a lake?' Even my dear old Navsari has the Dudiya and Sakariya lakes. I thought of turning back, but then it occurred to me that it was better to see it now rather than regret it later. Having come all this way, I might as well go inside. When you first enter the place, you are not able to make head or tail. We have already seen the underground wells which the Turks dig into the mountainsides, but this was on an altogether different scale. Its history can be traced to the times of the Byzantine emperors. There is no doubt that this lake must have been built at very great expense in those days. When we see the thousand marble columns that support the roof of this lake, we can estimate the scale of the cost. I could not understand why this structure was built at such great expense. It is possible that this expense was incurred so that it could be used as a source of water when the city was under siege. The kings of old and their skilled artisans seem to think very differently. The construction of an ordinary well these days involves a thousand engineers, while there is no shortage of such astounding structures in the city of Constantinople.

Sultan Valideh Bridge

After having spent the whole day taking in the sights of ancient Constantinople, a fun-loving traveller like me needed a change of mood. And luckily, there is such a place in the Turkish capital. Let us go and have a good time in the evening at the Sultan Valideh Bridge or the New Bridge. You may be extremely tired after a busy day, but if you spend half an hour here, you are bound to feel refreshed. People throng this bridge in such large numbers that it seems like the entire area is aswarm with insects. The crowds in their fashionable dresses certainly present a marvellous sight. There is an amazing variety of costumes on display. Here is a person wearing a white flowing dress in the Arab fashion and walking past him is a black Siddi from Africa. Turn your gaze and you will spot a resident of Bukhara with his distinctive headgear. And there you can spot a man who is wearing a tall hat in the Iranian style. And yonder is a European tourist hauling his huge camera behind him. Any traveller will be astounded by the huge variety of people one can see on this bridge. In Mumbai, one has to go to the Victoria Gardens for a fun time. But in Constantinople, you can stand in the middle of the Valideh Bridge and take in the breathtaking view of the Golden Horn. You will just not want to turn back. The golden rays of the setting sun bounce off the marble surfaces of the minarets, mosques and palaces to create a dazzling ambience that delights the heart. And if you turn to the other side, the greenery of the trees and the lush mountains and gardens are equally captivating. This beautiful bridge has been built on the creek of the Golden Horn and connects Galata to Istanbul. The bridge was built by Sultan Abdulmecid and was named after his mother, Sultan Valideh. It is about 420 metres long. If you work up an appetite by walking on the bridge, you can pop into any of the numerous stalls situated at both ends of the bridge, which sell coffee, tea and fruits. It is great fun to have a munch there. I was reminded of London Bridge when I was on this New Bridge. There is yet another bridge near the military harbour that spans this creek, known as the Old Bridge.

A New City

The bridge on which we had a good time in the evening leads to Galata and Pera, which are business districts. In Galata, one can find the main post office, banks, agencies of steamship companies, the custom house, and the offices of large business firms. You can also go to Galata from Istanbul by the tramway. There are three different ways by which one can go from Galata to Pera. The first is the Underground Cog Railway, which is also known as the Tunnel Railway. The second is the High Road, which is the route taken by the tramway. The third is a pedestrian pathway, which is the most fun of all. One has to climb 113 steps to get from Galata to Pera. The stairs are well constructed and broad enough for four men to walk on apace. They are lined by a variety of small shops. One has to be rather wary of these shopkeepers. They do not let you walk in peace. Here you find one of them calling out to you. There you have another who grips your hand and drags you towards his shop and asks you to buy something. The place seems to be noisier than the Machhiwad fish bazaar in Navsari. Not only are you out of breath as you climb those daunting stairs, but you also have to deal with such hassles. However, once you have crossed this stretch, you feel that you have been transported from hell to heaven. As Pera is mainly populated by Europeans, everything is organized in the European fashion. Its beautifully laid out roads are lined with large hotels and restaurants in which you can spot fashionable European ladies. Here are the names of a few hotels. The Pera Palace is a beautiful English hotel, while Hotel Bristol is opposite the Municipal Garden in Piccolo Campo. There is yet another big hotel known as the Grand. There are many European restaurants which are thronged by European travellers at night.

Turkish Hammam

Oh, my lord! This seems to be an altogether new thing. You better listen carefully so that there is no confusion. The Turkish hammam is one of the most attractive things in the Turkish capital and is the means to forget all your troubles and gladden your heart. If one returns from Constantinople without experiencing the joys of a hammam, one can be accused of having wasted the entire effort of travel. It is estimated that there are over two hundred hammams in the city catering to all classes of society. These places are regularly frequented by Turks in large numbers. It is indeed a blessing for those who have a heavy body, as the massage in these hammams makes the body feel very light. If one goes to a reputable hammam, one can see all patrons being subjected to a standard procedure. As one steps into the large reception hall, one can see ranks of servitors standing with their hands folded to their chests, as if they are waiting in anticipation for their next quarry. They bow deeply to welcome each new guest. I was not particularly taken in by their mock servility. The guest is expected to hand over all his clothes and wear a towel around his waist. A towel is also wrapped around his head. He also has to wear moccasins on his feet. After having donned this new costume, one is escorted by a servitor to an adjoining hall that is lined with rooms where one can wash oneself with hot or cold water. If one wants a massage before the bath, there are masseurs waiting in attendance who can give a very good massage. One can have a bath right away, or return to the reception hall and lie down on one of the mats laid out for this purpose as a servitor massages one's tired feet. If one feels like it, one can ask for a cup of tea or coffee. One is bound to leave the hammam with a light heart.

22

Return to England

On 19 July 1919, at eight o'clock in the night, I bid my final goodbyes to the Turkish capital. Our steamer *Sezby* set off into the ocean as the call of 'Allahu Akbar' resounded in the skies of Constantinople.

We had been stuffed in large numbers into this vessel as if we were goat and sheep. My dear Tommies were so excited about going home that they would listen to nobody and submit to no discipline. All through the night, they would steal away in twos to wander around the ship and chatter away. But under the circumstances, it was best to give these soldiers quite a lot of rein, or else they could get rather abusive. Such incidents were known to happen. Within the twinkling of an eye, we could see the mountains of Chanak. At eight in the morning, we docked into the port of Chanak and were marched into the embarkation camp.

Every soldier who was to be repatriated to England had to pass through this camp. They were given a very thorough medical examination, especially to detect any communicable diseases. If the symptoms of any such disease were detected, the soldier was not allowed to depart from the camp. Besides these medical tests, we had to waste seven days as we were put through a battery of procedures at this camp. On the 29th of July, we boarded yet another steamer, the *McDonald*. What was there to see on board? We were tired of gazing at the sky and the water. We were absolutely bored. It was as if our legs were bound together. But finally, we were approaching the Italian coastline. After a tiresome voyage of five days, everybody on board was delighted to be able to alight at this beautiful harbour.

However, in no time, our delight turned into despair. Someone screamed that the ship had run aground as it was entering the harbour. Someone else shouted that water was entering the ship. While these rumours were circulating, everybody scrambled to rush up to the deck. It was each man for himself as everybody tried to get a secure position. And then the news began to spread that the steamer had stopped as it awaited permission to enter the port of Taranto. How do the Italians manage to be as brilliant as this? One gets the answer as soon as one enters this port. A restraining wall has been built all around it, which keeps the ocean waters in check. The wall has a narrow entrance through which all ships enter. The gates of this opening present quite a frightening prospect as it seems like they can rip any passing vessel apart. When a large steamer exited through these gates, our hearts were in our mouths, wondering if the captain might make a very small error and ram into the restraining wall. It was quite a tight fit. When our vessel finally passed through, there was hardly a clearance of three or four feet between us and the wall. If the navigator had made the slightest error of judgement, our steamer would have broken into pieces and taken us all down with it. One is bound to mutter a few prayers for the engineers who built this marvel and hope that they rest in peace. If any traveller is passing through this region, he should certainly see this port.

Electric Railways on the Italian Mountains

Careful now! What have you seen that your mouth has popped open? This is the military camp at Taranto. It is quite a wonderful place. Why did the British build a huge military camp on a permanent footing in such a far-flung place? One cannot begin to estimate the amount of money that must have been spent to set up this camp. Anything one could have desired was available there. You could say that an entire city was present within the camp. Just outside it, the road was lined with large shops stocked with goods of the best Italian workmanship. Perhaps the most attractive objects were the Italian marble statues and vases. On reporting to the camp, the soldiers were treated to a concert by Italian musicians. It was all beyond my comprehension, but I must say they had very melodious voices.

For starters, these Italians looked just like my uncles and aunts, and I grew rather fond of them. Their features were very similar to those of the Parsis. Some of the Italian villagers really reminded me of our Parsi yokels. Their ears were pierced, from which dangled heavy gold earrings. But let us say goodbye to them and get back to our mail train.

After a long and tiresome wait of four days at Taranto, our train was ready to depart for France. It seemed to be made of very old rundown compartments. I was lucky to be in a bogie reserved for just twenty sergeants and a load of hammocks. Some of us spread these hammocks on the floor and used them as mattresses, while others slung them inside the compartment to make themselves comfortable. In the army, one has to make the best use of what is at hand rather than complain about the lack of something. You may not believe it, but there were two dining cars attached to the train. We could eat whenever we wanted on the running train. Besides, there were two more compartments which were the catering store. Every few hours, the train would stop at a station where we could stretch our legs for an hour or so. We first halted at Bari, and then marched into our camp in town where dining tables had been laid out for us and we were served a hot lunch. A band played on as we ate. Excellent arrangements had been made all through the route for the comfort of the soldiers. Bathing and washing facilities had been erected at major stations. Our Italian Mail left behind the famous cities of Italy and crossed the Alps.

If I were to write in detail about this journey, it would get rather boring. But I must warn you to be very careful if you are travelling in these parts. When the train halts at any station at night, you have to be on your guard as this country seems to be teeming with thieves. I will just mention one incident. When we were in deep slumber one night, a sergeant who was sleeping near an open window woke us all up with his screams. When we asked him what the matter was, he said that someone seemed to have nicked his overcoat and trousers. The rest of us burst out laughing. But what was to be done now? If only he could lay his hands on that scoundrel!

By then, we were inside French territory. Mashallah! After having traversed the length of Italy, I was back in France. At one time, this land was resounding with cannon fire, but now it felt like peace everywhere. I thought we would experience a little bit of the romance of France, but soon enough, our train pulled into the station at Boulogne. We idled here for four more days before we could board a ship which would take us across the English Channel. Indeed, the wheel of fortune seemed to have turned full circle. We would again get to spot the good old English policeman in his distinctive uniform patrolling the port of Dover from a distance. And the policeman would count himself fortunate as being the reason why the returning Tommies would shout and cheer.

British Army Ranks

What is the status of a British soldier? You might ask what a sergeant is, or whether a captain is a higher post than a major. Let me sort out this matter once and for all. The lowest position in the British Army is that of the private. He gets a salary of one shilling a day, that is, twelve annas in our currency. If he is found to be good enough, he gets promoted to the non-commissioned officer category. Once he has been examined, he is designated a lance corporal. He can now strut around wearing a stripe on his shoulder; but does that benefit him? He still gets the same salary. Only after he passes the next examination and becomes a corporal with two stripes does he get a salary hike: two and a half shillings. At the next level, he gets to be a good old sergeant. Can you imagine the power a sergeant wields in the regular army? God save us from him! Depending on his capabilities, a sergeant can become a quartermaster sergeant or a staff sergeant. The highest rank in the non-commissioned officer cadre is that of the warrant officer. You can become a sergeant major if you are very lucky. A sergeant major has more power over his men than even an officer. He can hand out severe punishments to an erring soldier: punish you if you sneeze, punish you if you walk, punish you for anything or ... nothing.

And now, we come to the ranks of the commissioned officers. The lowest rank is that of the second lieutenant who sports one star on his shoulder. The next grade is that of the lieutenant with two stars, followed by the captain who has the privilege of sporting three stars. A captain can become a company commander. The next rank is a major. A major sports a crown instead of stars on his shoulder and can become a senior company commander or the second in command of an entire platoon. Above the major is the lieutenant colonel who can be the commanding officer of a platoon. Wow! Does that not sound like a powerful position? It takes a long time for anyone to reach this rank.

But would it not be great if one could advance even further? The next rank is the brigadier who has command of a brigade and wears two crossed swords on his shoulder. Above the brigadier is the major general who wears a star in addition to the crossed swords. He can become the head of an entire division. Above him is the lieutenant general who has the honour of commanding a corps. And then you have the general, the field marshal, and finally, the commander in chief of the British empire. How much do you think they earn? Enough to empty out a treasury!

Post-War London

London! O London! What has become of you? How did this evil hour descend upon you? After the Great War, the situation in London seems to have deteriorated sharply. During the terrible times of the Great War, the soldiers were lionized and feted by members of the public who were attracted to them as if they were magnets. Upper-class ladies considered it a privilege to offer them a ride in their motor cars. And there were many instances when girls from reputed families would get married to one of these handsome soldiers in an urgently arranged ceremony. A few unfortunate soldiers would have to leave for the battlefields a few days after their wedding. They could be fighting in France, Egypt or Salonika. And since they were gone for a long time, their wives, whom they had married after a short romance of two or four days, would have no memories of them. When they returned home after the war, the soldiers would try to get together with their wives, but generally things did not work out. The ladies, whose frame of mind had completely changed during the war, had reverted to their original selves. They expected to live in a style befitting their family status. Instead of leading a happy married life, they were knocking on the doors of justice to escape these instant marriages. The soldier, who at one time was idolized, was now hungry and homeless. Such is the situation in London that nobody paid any attention to him. There are no jobs even for young men from upper-class families who are wasting their youth and intelligence by selling newspapers and flowers on the streets for a livelihood. The most unfortunate are those soldiers who have lost their limbs. You can see them sketching pictures on the roads or polishing boots in the hope of earning a few pence through the day.

After the conclusion of the war, the common populace has become rather vain. You can find a thirty-year-old woman proclaiming loudly with her nose in the air that it was her twelve-year-old son who won the year—because he was part of a mock battle of the Boy Scouts.

Young women who have stepped out of the army uniforms they wore during the war cannot forget the freedom of military life. You can spot them having a good time in pubs, drinking beer and smoking cigarettes in public. Though they may have donned their regular attire, the behaviour of these ladies has completely changed the complexion of London, much to the dismay of old-timers.

How Much Does it Cost to Stay in London?

Mere exaggeration! All kinds of numbers are bandied about by my countrymen. I am quite willing to admit that London is one of the most expensive places to visit in the world. After the Great War, the situation in London has worsened further, and the main reason for this state of affairs is the attitude of its residents.

During the war, they were used to enhanced wages and continue to expect the same even after its conclusion. The daily rates of London hotels hit the skies mainly because the number of hotels reduced drastically. But the situation is not as bad as some Indian tourists make it out to be. They are just throwing numbers in the air. One man claims to have spent five guineas a day to stay in London, while another coyly declares that he had to incur an expense of ten guineas daily. People in India are taken aback by such figures and wonder how much of it is true. I would say that one would have to make an allowance of ninety-nine per cent. Let me explain.

Three classes of people stay in London: the extremely rich and moneyed clans, the middling classes, and poor families. If one wants to give the impression of being a millionaire in London, then one has to obviously keep up pretences and spend lavishly. Otherwise it is not all that expensive. Besides expensive hotels, there are innumerable boarding houses in every London neighbourhood and they are available in a variety of standards. Even somebody like me could afford to stay in them. Let me give a few examples. The boarding houses in places like Victoria and Marylebone Road might be a tad expensive, with prices ranging from thirty-five shillings a week to as much as fifty shillings a week for full board. But if you are willing to venture a little further to places like Brixton or Stockwell Park Road, or to Hampstead and Highgate in North London, you could get a boarding house for as little as twenty shillings per week. It is not as if these houses are cramped. They are certainly much better than ours. You would get a comfortable room to sleep in, and use of the drawing room. However small the house, it is sure to have a piano. What more could one want? But most of our Indian visitors and students hesitate to venture into these neighbourhoods and end up spending a shilling where a penny would have sufficed. And they later badmouth the city when they return to India. I could comfortably stay in London for 150–200 rupees a month. Besides food and drink, I could visit a dancing hall once a week in this budget. But if you get involved with one of the local girls, like many of our countrymen are apt to do as soon as they arrive, these calculations will go for a toss. But why fault vilayat for such follies! Finally, the choice is up to you. You might be critical of my comments, but that does not detract from the truth.

23

A Final Goodbye

Why should I lie? When it was time for me to leave London, I did shed a few tears. It was obvious that there were conflicting emotions in my heart, a little regret, and not a little excitement. I was delighted to finally return to my dear native land after many years. On the other hand, I was rather disappointed to leave the colourful city of London behind.

Departure on the *SS Zeppelin*

We left the demobilization camp at Winchester to catch the nine o'clock night train to London. Our train chugged into the King's Cross railway station, from where we walked to the St Pancras station next door. Our train departed at 2.15 in the night and reached Liverpool the next morning at 9.30, where the White Star Line's steamship *Zeppelin* was ready and waiting for us.

The port of the business city of Liverpool seemed to be humming with activity and the coming and going of soldiers. Young women and girls were dancing to the tune of the Salvation Army band, which was also entertaining the long-distance passengers and soldiers. After high tea in the afternoon, the *Zeppelin* set forth with smoke billowing from its enormous chimneys and its booming whistles echoing all over Liverpool. It entered the sea among cries of 'Hurray!' from those on board. There were about two thousand passengers aboard the *Zeppelin*. About a thousand Indian soldiers were expected to join us at the French port of Marseilles, and an entire Indian platoon at Egypt. About five thousand of us who were on board this floating castle were going to alight on Indian soil. As our steamship *Zeppelin* had been built by German engineers, one can well imagine the various wondrous features on board. It was not as if the ship had been gifted by the Germans to their enemies. As it had not been designed in a straightforward manner, it would start bobbing at sea even though it had been under study and observation for over six months at the docks of a major American liner company. When we passed through the Bay of Biscay, which is famous for its storms, the passengers on board were traumatized by the rough seas. The dining tables were heaving wildly and no one was willing to go near them.

The Suez Canal

Ah! Why is it so hot here? After having just experienced the cool breezes of Europe, how can we handle this heat? All of us had been extremely eager to see the ship entering the Suez Canal, but before we realized it, the ship was already in the canal. May the soul of Ferdinand de Lesseps be blessed for having linked the two seas with this five-mile long canal. At 150 feet, it was wide enough for two steamers to pass each other. But the ten hours that it took for a ship to pass through it were very tiresome. The steamer huffed and puffed extremely slowly and it was also very hot. Neither could you sit inside the cabin, nor could you be on deck. The minute the ship entered the canal, no garbage could be thrown overboard. It was all accumulated at one corner of the deck where it stank to high heaven. Rotten potatoes and onions rolled around underfoot if we went up to the deck. We were eagerly waiting for a sight of the Red Sea. The European passengers on board the ship seemed to be rather bothered by the heat. They would have drinks of brandy and soda at short intervals to cool themselves down, or else it was a lemon scotch. Fun, isn't it? However, our minds were preoccupied. Nothing seemed to amuse us. We left the Red Sea behind and waved out to Aden from a distance.

A Final Goodbye

What? Why is everyone looking so refreshed? What are they so excited about? Friends, we were to reach Mumbai in the afternoon. The binoculars we held to our eyes were hurting the bridges of our noses, but that did not stop us. There was a strange excitement in the air. Our hearts were beating wildly. Patience! Patience! You might make fun of me now, but if you ever have this kind of experience, you will understand what I mean. Only a person who has been away for years from his dear motherland would understand what it means to be back home. To enter the Mumbai harbour once again and catch a glimpse of the famous Taj Mahal Hotel is enough to drive anyone crazy with happiness.

A...ll right! Goodbye, goodbye, and a final goodbye to my dear readers!

Finis

NARIMAN KARKARIA (1894–1949), a native of Navsari in Gujarat, enlisted in the British Army in London during the First World War. He saw action on three different fronts and participated in the Battle of the Somme and the conquest of Jerusalem. His Gujarati war memoir *Rangbhoomi par Rakhad*—the only First World War account written by an Indian to have been discovered thus far—was published in 1922. His only other book, *Iranbhoomi par Rakhad*, is an account of his year-long rambles in Iran and appeared in 1925. During the Second World War, he worked for the military training establishment at Ranchi. When he died in 1949, he was a major in the Indian Army.

MURALI RANGANATHAN is a Mumbai-based historian and translator. He researches the nineteenth century, with a special focus on Mumbai and western India. His current areas of interest include the Bombay Country Trade and printing history. His translation, from Marathi, of the iconic *Mumbaiche Varnan* was published in 2008 as *Govind Narayan's Mumbai: An Urban Biography from 1863*. He has edited and introduced *The Collected Works of J.V. Naik: Reform and Renaissance in Nineteenth Century Maharashtra* (2016) and *J.R.B. Jeejeebhoy's Bombay Vignettes: Explorations in the History of Bombay* (2018).

30 Years *of*

HarperCollins *Publishers* India

At HarperCollins, we believe in telling the best stories and finding the widest possible readership for our books in every format possible. We started publishing 30 years ago; a great deal has changed since then, but what has remained constant is the passion with which our authors write their books, the love with which readers receive them, and the sheer joy and excitement that we as publishers feel in being a part of the publishing process.

Over the years, we've had the pleasure of publishing some of the finest writing from the subcontinent and around the world, and some of the biggest bestsellers in India's publishing history. Our books and authors have won a phenomenal range of awards, and we ourselves have been named Publisher of the Year the greatest number of times. But nothing has meant more to us than the fact that millions of people have read the books we published, and somewhere, a book of ours might have made a difference.

As we step into our fourth decade, we go back to that one word – a word which has been a driving force for us all these years.

Read.